LONGS PEAK

a Rocky Mountain chronicle

by
Stephen Trimble

International Standard Book Numbers:
0-930487-17-6 softbound
0-930487-18-4 hardbound
Library of Congress Card Catalog Number pending
First edition: 8000 softbound
2000 hardbound

Coordination: Glen Kaye, Marjorie Dunmire
Design: Christina Watkins
Production: Nancy Curtis, Jim Carter
Printing: Lahey Printing Company, Denver, Colorado

CONTENTS

For the mountain.

For everyone who has climbed Longs Peak—
or dreamed of climbing it.

And for my parents, Isabelle and Don Trimble,
who taught me to love both mountains and books.

Many people helped with this book. I thank them all. Chief Naturalist Glen Kaye of Rocky Mountain National Park comes first. He initiated the project and consistently offered perceptive criticism, enthusiasm, and logistical cooperation throughout my research and writing. Other staff members at Rocky Mountain National Park contributed their time, ideas, and editorial comments. They include Ferrell Atkins, Marj Dunmire, Bob Howard, Charlie Logan, and Phil Zichterman. Nature Association Board Member Lennie Bemiss helped with local history.

The following sharp-eyed critics generously reviewed early drafts of the manuscript: A. William Alldredge, David Armstrong, Richard Beidleman, Audrey Benedict, Jim Benedict, Bill Forrest, Robert Johnson, Don Trimble, Isabelle Trimble, and Christina Watkins. Jennifer Dewey, in particular, inspired me to keep on in hot pursuit of simplicity and clarity. In the end, of course, all responsibility for accuracy lies with me.

Mac Dings, Bill Forrest, Enda Mills Kiley, and Merrill Mattes talked to me about their experiences on the mountain. Jennifer Dewey, David Johnson, and Kathy Kelley assisted with field work. My friend and editor Rick Stetter showed great tolerance when I postponed other work to complete this book.

I owe my affection for Longs Peak to three experiences. Growing up in Denver, I watched the mountain change with the seasons, and my parents, Isabelle and Don Trimble, taught me to pay attention to such things. Richard Beidleman, Dennis Lynch, and Ann Zwinger nourished my interest in Front Range ecology during the years I attended Colorado College. And David Johnson, Lance Williams, and I climbed many Colorado mountains together.

S. T.
Jaconita, New Mexico
April, 1984

LONGS PEAK

MOUNTAIN SPIRIT

LONGS PEAK begins as an expectation, a dream of the shining Rockies in the minds of weary prairie travelers. The mountain becomes real where the Rocky Mountains first become visible from the Great Plains. Finally, it is there, when a moment before it wasn't.

Arriving at the mountains after the long trip across the plains is like reaching shore after a lengthy voyage. In this way Longs Peak serves as guidepost, like Gibraltar or the white chalk cliffs of Dover. Its bold East Face looks down upon grasslands for more than a hundred miles.

Longs stands as vanguard of the mountains, northernmost 14,000-foot peak in the Rockies, with Pikes Peak and Mount Evans one of three landmark high points of the Front Range. All three peaks can be seen from Denver, but Longs holds a special place. Pikes Peak really is Colorado Springs' mountain. Mount Evans blends with other peaks on the western horizon. Northward, however, behind Mount Meeker, the unmistakable blocky summit of Longs Peak rises, smoke-blue in summer, ice-white in winter.

Highways reach the summits of Pikes and Evans. But Longs stands far above roads, a *climb* that requires using your hands even on the easiest route. If a prophet were looking for a peak to retreat to, if a god were looking for a perch from which to toss thunderbolts at the people of the plains, neither would charter a ride up Pikes or Evans. They surely would stride to the top of Longs Peak.

Longs Peak has every quality that makes mountains memorable. Even with 10,000 people striving for its summit each year, the mountain's wilderness quality remains intact—for it lies within Rocky Mountain National Park, and no road will ever civilize its upper flanks. The mountain's distinctive silhouette is visible for great distances. It is high: 14,255 feet. For rock climbers, the Diamond, central wall of the East Face of Longs Peak, has the same glamour as El Capitan in Yosemite.

Immediately below the Diamond, Chasm Lake reflects Longs Peak in a perfect fusion of water, mountain, and sky—one of the classic images of the Rockies, like the Maroon Bells at Maroon Lake or the Grand Teton and Mount Moran from Jackson Lake. Longs dominates the other most-reproduced views in Rocky Mountain National Park: that from Bear Lake, and the great sweep from Trail Ridge Road across the gulf of Forest Canyon.

Centuries before Major Stephen Long spotted the mountain in 1820, Native Americans knew Longs Peak, from unnamed bands of mammoth hunters to historic Arapaho and Ute. They named it, oriented their travels by it, and trapped eagles on its summit.

In the first half of the nineteenth century, official explorers and journal-keeping tourists tramped along the base of the Southern Rockies below the great conical peak seen by Long and known by his name as early as 1825. They made public the West that the Indian and mountain man carried in their heads.

Within forty years of Major Long's adventure, settlers were pouring into Colorado. William N. Byers, editor of Denver's *Rocky Mountain News*, was doing his best to demystify the local wilderness by trying for the first recorded ascent of Longs Peak. In 1864, he reached Mount Meeker, but failed to conquer Longs. In 1868, Byers joined forces with John Wesley Powell's homemade "Rocky Mountain Scientific Exploring Expedition" to gain the Longs Peak summit.

Powell—soon to be a national hero after his river exploration through the Grand Canyon—combined a passion for facts with a romantic eye for awesome scenery. Just beginning his long career as scientist and arid lands prophet, Longs was Powell's first "first." But already he approached this mountain with a critical balance.

Just to stand on the summit was important; the one-armed major clambered up the tricky route with the rest of the party. Before the descent, Powell gathered the little group and spoke formally of the significance of their achievement. And he posted two college-student assistants along the ridge to take hourly barometric readings for a week, collecting basic elevation and weather data for the region.

Powell understood the nature of mountains. Just as a rock climber on the Diamond balances delicately on subtle foot and handholds, fact and spirit balance to make Longs Peak.

Anna Dickinson, first woman to climb Longs Peak, also understood this balance. She wrote of sitting around a treeline campfire with the Hayden Survey party in 1871 after the climb:

> . . . talking of many things—strange stories of adventure in the mountains and gorge, climbs through which a score of times life had suspended simply on strength of fingers, nice poise on a hand ledge thrust out into eternity, wild tales of frontier struggles, intricacies of science, discussions of human life and experience in crowded cities, devotion and enthusiasm shown in any cause—all things, in fact that touch the brain and soul, the heart and life, of mortals who really live, and do not merely exist. A talk worth climbing that height to have . . .

Mountain facts—Anna Dickinson's "intricacies of science"—are never solitary. The give and take of erosion and uplift define Longs Peak as a landform—as a summit in the Front Range of the Southern Rocky Mountains of north-central Colorado, a mile and a half east of the Continental Divide. Wind, temperature, topography, precipitation, and sunlight interplay to map a mosaic of plant communities.

Mountain spirit invigorates the light streaming through the Keyhole and onto the snowy Boulder Field in winter. It lives in clouds enveloping the summit and in lightning striking the Keyboard of the Winds. In the chirp of a pika, the coolness of granite under fingertips, the smell of fir needles after a rain shower.

Mountain spirit has much to do with mountain facts—with facts *perceived* by people, and transformed into feelings. Lying somewhere between fact and spirit, between the tangible and the intangible, is time: balanced at any single moment are all the factors which make Longs Peak.

"... in one's imagination it grows to be much more than a mountain."

Isabella Bird, 1879.

Each aspect of Longs Peak amplifies understanding of every other. To learn its glacial history makes the Diamond even more impressive. To face into a wind too fierce to walk against makes more vivid the struggles of tundra flowers. To sit eye to eye with a ptarmigan, see bistort bobbing in the wind, and to sense the power in a storm building over the Divide—these experiences make facts live.

Longs Peak embodies the balance—and the tension—between wildness and civilization. From as far as downtown Denver, we feel the energy of this interchange at a glance. Looking up to the mountain, we see storms playing freely over its summit. The amount of snow on its flanks marks the passing seasons. From skyscrapers and asphalt we can make contact with this great peak.

As we try to unite our rational and intuitive halves, no better catalysts exist than mountains like Longs Peak. To comprehend this mountain, we must balance fact with experience, science with art, geological time with moment by moment huffing and puffing up the trail. We must give our time and energy, thought and sweat.

In return, Longs Peak can teach us any principle of its natural history we wish to understand. It can tell stories of human tragedy and transcendence. The mountain also can put our fleeting sparks of lives in perspective against the profound vastness of geologic time.

When we stand on its summit, we share with Longs Peak a connection between earth and sky, a bond that runs through us from cloud to mountain. The experience transfigures our awareness. For a moment, in balance, we comprehend the mountain as a whole.

chapter one

MOUNTAIN OF ROCK

LEAN back against a rock warmed by the blazing alpine sun—in the Boulder Field, on the shelving rim of Chasm Lake, or on the summit of Longs itself. You are in touch with the skin, flesh, and bones of the peak, for this is a mountain made from rock. The higher you go, the more the rock dominates, until above treeline the helmeted summit block rises bare of all but the tiniest plants.

Every boulder encapsulates the story of the mountain—in the mineral crystals which give each its texture, in the events which raised to this lofty altitude the layers from which each boulder has weathered. To trace the odyssey of this mountain of rock takes us far from Colorado—and far into the past. On this journey continents rift apart, crash together, and drift about the planet. Time ticks second by deliberate second through nearly two billion years. Life evolves from its beginnings in ancient seas to the lushness and diversity of modern forests and meadows.

Somehow a single piece of granite will survive eons of these cosmic forces to absorb solar heat on a summer's day and transmit it to the chilled skin of an individual member of a recently evolved mammalian species. No survival could be more moving.

Massive and awesome rock —the skin, flesh, and bones of the peak.

GENESIS: THE ANCIENT ROCK.

The Precambrian rock that makes Longs Peak is as ancient as the rock at the bottom of the Grand Canyon. To *feel* just how ancient takes effort. Imagine the 4.6 billion years of earth history as a single year. The earth formed on the first of January. The present is the last instant before midnight on the thirty-first of December.

On this scale, the oldest Longs Peak rock formed in mid-May. We know very little about what happened before then. The Precambrian Era—this mysterious time before complex life developed—continued until mid-November. Dinosaurs appeared in mid-December and disappeared the day after Christmas. The last two thousand years span the fourteen seconds before midnight on New Year's Eve.

Geologists learn to think in terms of billions of years, speaking about a mere one or two million years as we speak of hours. John McPhee, in *Basin and Range,* quotes one geologist's method of reconciling brief human lifetimes with "deep time," of achieving "a kind of companionship with the earth":

> If you free yourself from the conventional reaction to a quantity like a million years, you free yourself a bit from the boundaries of human time. And then in a way you do not live at all, but in another way you live forever.

Longs Peak rocks record a distant part of such "deep time"—a chronicle beginning more than 1.75 billion years ago. Continents had developed but in unknown relation to each other. Life already had existed for more than a billion years (some paleontologists say two billion), but had evolved no farther than bacteria and algae. The continents remained barren for a billion years more, until the atmosphere developed to shield life on land from the sun's fatal ultraviolet radiation.

Sediments—from ancient streams, lakes, and oceans of which we know nothing—gradually became buried deep within the earth, where heat and pressure began changing them to harder rocks. Twice, about 1,725 million years ago, and again about 1,400 million years ago, the deeply buried rocks again were transfigured by folding, heat, and pressure, this time associated with molten rock (magma) rising into them from beneath.

Each time powerful earth forces reworked the ancient sediments, and each time they became further "metamorphosed." Finally, they became the metamorphic rocks called schist and gneiss. The molten masses of invading magma gradually cooled and crystallized into granite, here and there shot through with similar, but coarser-grained pegmatite.

Today, the swirls and spirals of Longs Peak's schist and gneiss testify to mighty forces at work as they formed and reformed deep within a Precambrian continent. These metamorphic rocks—dark, with a fine-grained glitter—erode into jagged teeth, like the Keyboard of the Winds between Longs Peak and Pagoda Mountain.

Longs Peak granite dates to the second great invasion of magma— 1.4 billion years ago. Made of glassy quartz crystals, sharp-edged pink and white rectangles of feldspar, and tiny mirrors of black or white mica, it erodes into smooth domes like those around Granite Pass, and makes up the core of the mountain, including the naked wall of the East Face. On a cliff above the Ship's Prow at Chasm Lake, granite and schist alternate in stripes of monumental scale.

Granite around the peak differs in mineral content and crystal size. Geologists have distinguished ten varieties, including very coarse-grained granite on Mount Lady Washington, the snow-white granite of

Banded metamorphic schist and gneiss erode in jagged teeth, like the Keyboard of the Winds strung between Longs Peak and Pagoda Mountain.

Pagoda Mountain, and a granite with garnet clusters on Longs itself.

The Precambrian Era—the enormous span of time ending about 570 million years ago—gave Longs Peak the rocks that form its geologic vocabulary. Its revolutionary events happened so long ago they seem of a single age—simply "ancient." How can we conceive of the real difference between 1,725 and 1,400 million years?

Perhaps we never can.

SILENCE, SEAS, *and* SAND. Of events during the 870 million years following creation of the Longs Peak granite, the mountain is silent. No rocks in the vicinity tell the story of this gap—the end of the Precambrian Era and a bit of the succeeding era, nearly twenty percent of all earth history.

The two eras of earth history that followed the Precambrian, the Paleozoic and Mesozoic, wrote their chapters in detail over the succeeding 500 million years. But the mountain has shoved their record aside in its rise with the Rockies. Rocks from these eras flank the Front Range, but were eroded from its top as it rose. Longs Peak as we see it today is carved from ancient rock, but by near-contemporary sculptors.

Throughout these 500 million years, oceans swept back and forth across what would become Colorado. About 300 million years ago a mountain range rose—the Ancestral Rockies, related to distant movements of the crustal plates as the early continents changed position during huge expanses of time. Within a few million years the Ancestral Rockies were eroded flat. Sahara-sized dunes covered the land, to be inundated by the sea once more.

Life swirled in the oceans, growing ever more complex, then ventured onto the continents. Mammals arose more than 200 million years ago. Flowering plants appeared not long after—in the mid-Mesozoic—and began to dominate while mammals still scurried in the shadows of dinosaurs.

As the Mesozoic neared its end—some 65-75 million years ago— great changes swept over the planet. The earth we know began to rough out. The early supercontinent Pangea had split apart, and its fragments were approaching inch by inch the map of "the world" we take for granted. Dinosaurs disappeared. Mammals came into their own.

And from Canada to Mexico the Rocky Mountains began to take shape, displacing the ocean from Colorado for the last time—so far.

On the geologic time scale these revolutionary events happened in a moment. They took ten million years to hit their stride. The ocean dawdled for 16 million years before leaving all of Colorado. Another 60 million years sufficed to produce what we think of as this unchanging mountain.

We could have recognized Longs Peak in rough outline for only the last five million years—after its fault block rose above surrounding ridges. Not until the geological yesterday did glaciers gouge the mountain into its familiar angular form.

RISE OF THE ROCKIES.

The flat, bouldery five-acre summit of Longs Peak constitutes one of the fascinating controversies of Rocky Mountain geology. It clearly is a remnant of an unglaciated ancient upland. But just how ancient?

Its granite gradually has risen from deep within the earth to this present eminent height. Erosion planed it flat; uplift preserved it while lower flanks of the mountain passed through successive burial in sediment, re-exposure, and glaciation. We know a great deal about these cycles of uplift and erosion. But during *which* cycle of erosion the flat summit of the mountain developed remains unclear.

Uplift and erosion are twin forces. Uplift steepens stream gradients, increasing erosion. If erosion keeps pace, stripping away sediment from high country and carrying it off to low country at the same rate as uplift, mountains rise structurally but not in elevation. Uplift must exceed erosion to increase the height of the peaks.

The summit of Longs Peak lies more than 20,000 feet above similar Precambrian rocks buried beneath the plains. If we add the thickness of Precambrian layers already eroded from the top of Longs Peak, the grand total adds up to more than five miles of uplift.

It happened in tiny increments, in pulses. Layers bowed upward as crustal forces elevated the land. Faults—those lines along which blocks of rock give way to release unimaginable stresses—moved a few inches or feet at a time, once every couple of centuries. Distant jostling of crustal plates—one plate plunging beneath another, the opening of oceans—affected each event in the growing Rockies·in ways we do not fully understand.

The Front Range did not begin its rise until 67.5 million years ago. By the end of the Mesozoic about 65 million years ago, streams already had eroded some 8,500 feet of sedimentary rock from the rising mountains, exposing their Precambrian core. This original mountain-building phase (called the Laramide Orogeny) continued until 54 million years ago, blocking out the major ranges of the Rockies. Laramide uplift totaled 20,000 feet or more—revolutionizing the landscape at an average rate of only an inch and three-quarters rise per century.

About 50 million years ago Laramide uplift slowed to a halt. The eroded mountain blocks merged eastward with the plains in a gentle slope. The next 15 million years were quiet; with little uplift or erosion, weathering took over. The elements worked on exposed bedrock, break-

16

Preserved through millions of years of upheavals, the flat granite summit of Longs Peak gives the mountain its distinctive silhouette, geologists a tantalizing puzzle, and climbers a welcome resting place.

From Chasm View, a hiker looks down Roaring Fork gorge, its glacier-scoured basins holding the tarns of Chasm Lake and Peacock Pool.

ing it into ever smaller pieces, chemically attacking its minerals. In combination with plants, weathering converted rock into soil.

This deeply weathered 40-million-year-old surface is preserved in some places. Some geologists believe one such place is the summit of Longs Peak. Others believe the flat summit was cut much more recently.

Uplift resumed again after this time, raising the old plain—and destroying most of it in renewed erosion. Time passed. Uplift and erosion seesawed. Volcanic ash poured out from volcanoes in the Never Summer Range and from vents still further to the west, burying all but the highest mountains.

With subsequent intermittent uplift, erosion by water and wind stripped away most of the ash. A series of small uplifts continued until 5-7 million years ago, when the mountains stood just 8,000 feet high—barely above the plains on either side. This broad erosional surface is another key Front Range feature, preserved here and there despite subsequent upheavals.

Finally, with extensive uplift beginning about 5-7 million years ago and continuing today, the land reached its current elevation. Erosion increased apace, cutting canyons and highlighting hogbacks flanked by linear valleys. These latter beds, tilted sharply at the rising edge of the mountains, remain conspicuous along the eastern foot of the Front Range from Colorado Springs to Fort Collins.

Many faults have existed in nearly the same places for millions of years. They may reverse the direction of their movement, but move they must, earthquake after earthquake, era after era. Some geologists think the Southern Rockies rose where the Ancestral Rockies—and even Precambrian mountain ranges—had risen before them, along lines determined by venerable Precambrian faults.

Glaciation has added sharply-drawn refinements, but the last great regional uplift sketched in the modern landscape, reshuffling blocks between faults. Ancient upland surfaces capping some blocks rose high. Others held their own in elevation. Still others dropped, to be buried by fresh sediments in river valleys.

The difficulty of guessing the age of a patch of rolling upland along the top of the range—like the flat summit of Longs Peak—begins to come clear. Does it date to the recent plains of 5 million or 40 million years ago? Or did it develop between these dates?

Few geologists place the erosional antiquity of the flat summit of Longs Peak beyond 40 million years. However, some suggest that it preserves a bit of some truly ancient surface, the roots of the Ancestral Rockies, or the ground-down 600-million-year-old surface of Precambrian mountains. Either way, the summit of the peak has stood at what geologist Gerald Richmond calls the "roof of the Rockies" for longer than the mountain itself has existed.

A GLACIOLOGY PRIMER.

We live in the Pleistocene Ice Age. Although geologists have designated the 10,000 years since the last major glaciation as the Holocene Epoch, this may only be a time between glaciers, the most recent *interglacial* in a cycle of glacial events that spans the last several million years.

What *is* a glacier? What makes one mass of permanent ice officially a glacier and another a mere snowfield? Does the gleaming white backdrop to Chasm Lake deserve to be called "Mills Glacier?"

Here is the definition in one breath: alpine glaciers form when permanent snowpack recrystallizes to form dense ice and deepens to the point where it flows downhill.

Here is the definition, step-by-step. Climate is crucial—for winter snow must last from year to year. Complex snow crystals gradually recrystallize into simple granular ice crystals of uniform size called *névé*. Water vapor escapes from compacting névé, meltwater trickles down and refreezes in lower layers, and the added pressure of new snowfall forces out air. Névé becomes ice.

With enough pressure (the weight of about 160 feet of ice), lower layers begin to flow like plastic: the icefield becomes a glacier. Flowing ice carries the upper, brittle layers along like a raft, shattering it in *crevasses* as the glacier moves over uneven ground. Glaciers rarely move more than a few centimeters in a day. The bottom and sides, retarded by friction as they grind past the surrounding rock, move more slowly than the center.

But move they do, and in doing so, they grind and pry, quarry and polish—incorporating resulting rock debris into the glacier. They transform valley cross-sections from V's to U's. They eat into headwalls, where meltwater freezes in cracks at night, steepening the sides of half-bowl-shaped *cirques* to supreme verticality, like the East Face of Longs Peak. They scour basins in bedrock, which fill with water after glaciers retreat, forming *tarns* like Chasm Lake, Peacock Pool, and the lakes of Glacier Gorge.

Rock debris in the moving ice accumulates along the sides or is carried to the end of the glacier. Mills Moraine is a *lateral moraine* left along the north margin of the Roaring Fork glacier as it retreated toward Longs's East Face. The *end moraine* below Longs Peak Campground proves this glacier once reached almost to the floor of Tahosa Valley at today's Colorado Highway 7: only the glacier could have left this ridge of rounded boulders and pebbles.

Glaciers affect the landscape most powerfully by quarrying. The Diamond is not so much carved, as excavated—block by block. Where the Roaring Fork glacier lay against its headwall, a great crevasse developed where it pulled away from the cliff as the ice began to flow.

Pleistocene glaciers left the X-shaped ridges of Longs Peak and its surrounding summits standing high above streams of ice. Glaciers lay against the mountain in the valleys of Roaring Fork (Mills Glacier), Hunters Creek (merging with Wild Basin Glacier), and in Glacier Gorge and Boulder Brook (merging with Bartholf Glacier in Glacier Basin).

This *bergschrund* allowed meltwater to constantly trickle into cracks in the cliff during warm days, freeze at night, and break off rock for the glacier to remove.

A complex fracture system, oriented just right by sheer chance, allowed quarrying to proceed to remarkable extremes, paring the Diamond clean while gravity steepened it. Glacial ice and meltwater removed the debris. The staggering East Face is the result.

CYCLES OF ICE.

No one can envision tomorrow with certainty. Nor can they see into the distant past without doubts. With enough knowledge of the past, however, we can attempt to predict the future.

Longs Peak could yet lose its flat summit to rejuvenated glaciers in the next few thousand years and sharpen to the converging point of a Matterhorn.

Glaciers become likely as continents rise in elevation and cluster near the poles—as they do today. Such long-term trends linked to continental drift seem responsible for glaciers in other eras—evident even in Precambrian time—and for cooling of the world climate in the last 38 million years. In this most recent cooling cycle, glaciers developed as early as 10 million years ago on high-latitude uplands. The Pleistocene Epoch, or Great Ice Age, began about two million years ago.

Such gradual shifts in climate over millions of years do not explain alternate advance and retreat of glaciers on a scale of mere thousands of years. Today, scientists couple these cycles of Pleistocene ice with the changing geometry of the earth's orbit.

The annual seasonal cycle from freshening spring to frigid winter depends on the earth's distance from the sun and on the tilt of its axis. Small, regular variations in these form the basis of the *astronomical theory of glaciation*. The earth's orbit alternates from circular to elliptical. Its axis simultaneously wobbles and changes its angle of tilt. These nuances make winters milder or more severe and summers cooler or warmer—climatic changes obviously important to a growing or melting glacier.

In testing this theory, scientists have found remarkable correspondence between astronomical calculations, climatic records in deep-sea drill cores, and glacial deposits. Changes in the earth's orbit may indeed cause glaciers to form, advance, and retreat. And all indications point to a much colder world in the next few tens of thousands of years. In trying to understand the past, predict the future, and comprehend our brief lifetimes within the current climatic cycle, we reach out from Longs Peak far into space and time.

Much current research in Rocky Mountain glaciology aims at clarifying the number of advances of glacial ice, and the absolute dates

"...you go up...
on all fours...
You come down
on all fives..."

William Allen White, 1946.

of each. Traditionally, late Pleistocene glacial advances were expected to fit neatly into three cycles, pre-Bull Lake, Bull Lake, and Pinedale advances, separated by warm interglacial periods. The Pleistocene supposedly ended with retreat of the Pinedale glaciers about 10,000 years ago.

But this elegant and simple scheme gets more complex with every bit of new information added. First came recognition of glacial advances *since* the Pinedale. The Ice Age did not end with the official end of the Pleistocene, so this called for a new term—the Little Ice Age or *Neoglacial* ("new" glacial). Next came finer and finer divisions of each major glacial advance.

As in so much of science, sharply defined terms break down as we learn more and more of continuous natural processes. These problems all turn up in tracing the glacial history of Longs Peak.

Most ranges show only Bull Lake, Pinedale, and Neoglacial deposits, with several advances attributable to each. Mapping these invisible glaciers grows more difficult with increasingly tangled topography. Every valley had its own glaciers, and each advance of ice destroyed traces of the one before it.

Dating techniques further amplify—and complicate—our understanding. Geologists compare different degrees of soil development, boulderiness, and weathering to sequence the layers of morainal debris overlaying one another. These clues to *relative time* tell us most of what we know about the order of events in the past. But they tell us nothing about actual dates, *absolute time.*

Today sophisticated methods measuring radioactive decay of one element to another reveal the approximate number of years elapsed since formation of rocks. Alternative techniques seem even more startling. Pollen cores from bogs record vegetational history which can be radiocarbon-dated. Lichens growing slowly at known rates on moraines fresh from Neoglacial time give us another measure of absolute age.

When radioactive dating methods first became popular, geologists confidently set up timetables for each glacial advance. But dates published in the mid-1970s proved hopelessly wrong within a decade. Future dating no doubt will throw our current glacial time brackets again in disarray. To establish a calendar for glacial events on Longs Peak—however tenuously—think back about 140,000 years ago to envision one stage of Bull Lake glaciation, and about 18,000-20,000 years ago for the last major Pinedale glaciation.

But treat such specific numbers gingerly. They are fragile glimpses into the story of Longs Peak; their precision is an illusion. They are bound to change.

SCOOPING OUT THE MOUNTAIN.

Picture the flat summit of Longs Peak extending outward, continuous with other uplands. Over several million years this scene changes. Uplift forces streams to cut downward and headward, fragmenting the rolling surface. With a cooling climate, glaciers develop. They widen valley floors and steepen walls, eat back into the upland, and scoop out half-bowls at valley heads. One remnant of the upland surface becomes more and more isolated—reduced to the small acreage at the summit of the mountain.

In simplest form, this is the glacial story of Longs Peak.

The earliest glaciers detectable in Rocky Mountain National Park deposited debris about 160,000 years ago east of Longs Peak in Tahosa Valley. Another patch of such pre-Bull Lake glacial debris flanks North St. Vrain Creek south of Meeker Park. Still earlier glaciations have left no clues visible through intervening readvances of ice.

Younger, intermediate-age glaciers of the Bull Lake stage left strong marks on Longs Peak as they deepened to a maximum of 2,000 feet. Ice steepened the ridges surrounding the mountain, gouging into the peak from the four directions. And then—like all glacial advances—the Bull Lake glaciers retreated as the climate warmed.

In Bull Lake time, two advances left moraines along the valleys of Roaring Fork and Alpine Brook. The first Bull Lake moraine highlights the upper end of Jims Grove. The later Bull Lake advance left a great bulky lobe of debris just south of Longs Peak Ranger Station, where Roaring Fork canyon issues from the mountain front at about 9,000 feet above sea level.

Pinedale glaciers pushed even farther down Longs Peak than did Bull Lake ice. They steepened, deepened, and finished the sculpture of the modern mountain. A Pinedale moraine breaches the broader Bull Lake moraine and extends in a narrow tongue east of the park boundary along the Roaring Fork to 8,800 feet—almost to the highway in Tahosa Valley. Both Bull Lake and Pinedale glaciers helped build Mills Moraine—the lateral moraine along the north side of Roaring Fork.

On the north slope of Longs Peak, a lobe of ice extended down Boulder Brook valley. In Glacier Basin it joined the ice stream flowing through Glacier Gorge from the west face of Longs Peak. Southward, glacial ice lay against the mountain in the Hunters Creek drainage, merging with North St. Vrain Glacier in Wild Basin.

Imagine today's friendly green valleys filled with rivers of barren ice. Picture the glaciers streaming from the island mountaintop, blue-white ice marked with dark lines of morainal debris and a fretwork of black crevasses. In lowlands, cold winds blew past browsing mammoths. Each time the glaciers waned, torrents of meltwater opaque with rock scourings poured down foothill canyons.

The X-shaped ridges of Longs and its surrounding summits remained high above this network of glaciers. Today, they stand even higher above the valley floors. Longs Peak naturalist and historian Paul Nesbit condensed the geography of the mountain into a single phrase: ". . . the peak is four-square."

Longs Peak rises at the crosspoint. Mount Meeker on the southeast ridge is second-highest, at 13,911 feet. Pagoda Mountain, to the southwest, comes next at 13,497 feet, followed by Storm Peak (northwest ridge) at 13,326 and Mount Lady Washington (northeast ridge) at 13,281 feet. The higher and narrower of these rocky spines form beautiful examples of *aretes*, ridges steepened to airy catwalks by glaciers gnawing from either side.

Once recession began, Pinedale glaciers several miles long and 1,500 feet thick disappeared in as little as 2,000 years. The Front Range may have lost its Pinedale ice by about 15,000 years ago. Several small advances in the last 10,000 years have left minor moraines above Chasm Lake and in the Boulder Field. Mills Glacier is a remnant of these "Little Ice Ages." Today a stagnant icefield, it flows no longer—a glacier no more.

Glacier lily

HEAVING ROCKS *and* FLOWING SOIL.

Glaciers, helped by frost-wedging, have created large-scale landforms on Longs Peak: cirques, U-shaped valleys, aretes, moraines. But frozen water has no need to coalesce into rivers of ice to transform this land. Small-scale landforms on the mountain also owe most of their personality to ice.

Every water droplet that crystallizes at night nudges a bit of earth or a pebble. When water freezes and expands, it exerts a power of 30,000 pounds per square inch. Frost action smooths rough edges from the high tundra just as it quarries cliffs smooth. Ann Zwinger expressed it well in *Land Above the Trees*:

> . . . alpine tundra is more rolling and gentle than one somehow expects . . . It has a well-scrubbed, well-worn look, like an old table top perhaps, once painted nicely green, now warped, faded to a patina, chips of paint remaining only in the cracks.

A mountainside open to the alpine climate is as naked as flesh. Exposed human skin will freeze in two minutes on an average winter's day on the peak. The rocky alpine skin of the mountain endures the same inexorable power.

Frost breaks bedrock into fragments and covers gentle slopes with

Water carves Longs Peak—buffeting the dark rock of Roaring Fork, saturating soil along the creek through Chasm Meadow, freezing, prying, and nudging the cliffs of Ship's Prow.

boulderfields (*felsenmeers*—"seas of rock"). Soil expands as it freezes then settles as it thaws, moving downslope at a creep where it overlays bedrock. When saturated with meltwater, soil flows over frozen ground in a process called *solifluction*.

Today, Longs Peak tundra is too dry for solifluction to occur widely. It moves soil downslope only during spring thaw just below long-lasting snowbanks. Permafrost is rare. With extensive impermeable bedrock and dry soils, expect permafrost on Longs Peak only under wet soils blown free of snow in winter. Frost creep dominates soil movement throughout modern Front Range tundra.

Soil creeping downhill under frost-power heaves out boulders and stones, scattering them across the tundra in *patterned ground*. Rock streams line gullies; stone-banked terraces drape garlands of blocky debris across slopes. On the level, boulders form networks of circles and polygons. Annual freeze-thaw cycles, not daily ones, accomplish frost-heaving of larger stones.

Once thought to initiate development of cirques, it now seems that semi-permanent snowbanks in depressions act more on the soil downslope. In a process called *nivation*, they greatly increase sediment loss through a continuous flow of meltwater during summer.

Today, all of these processes operate at a fraction of their potential strength, in an interplay determined by the level of the water-table and the slope of each ridge. Important heaving takes place only in the upper 15-25 inches of soil; the annual average downslope soil movement measures a maximum of little over an inch.

In snow-accumulation areas solifluction still can overwhelm the effects of frost-sorting, mixing stones and soil in turf-banked lobes and terraces. Where deep snow protects terraces in winter, dense vegetation covers them. Shallower snow-cover allows frost hummocks to develop.

With still shallower snowpack, bitter winter winds kill plants on the tops of hummocks, creating bare frost boils. Frost heaves out stones from the top of the eroded scars of these boils, moving rocks up to a foot in a single season and building up rock rings which plants invade. Pioneer plants, in turn, rebuild soil until the hummock rises once more—and begins the cycle anew.

THE WATER MOUNTAIN. Water

carves—and has carved—Longs Peak. In its recent history, the changing climate has brought more and more effective water power to the mountain—a long series of buffetings by frost-action, streams of ice, and freshets of glacial meltwater.

Today, Longs Peak snowfields water Great Plains farms and suburban lawns. Mountain watersheds allow the existence of cities in the

 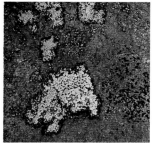

First touch of life to take hold in the wake of retreating glaciers, lichens pattern this mountain from summit to base, reintroducing life to freshly scarred rock.

semiarid West. Twenty percent of Colorado's streamflow comes from the five percent of its area above treeline. Understanding the glacial past—and future—is not merely the esoteric domain of scientists. If glaciers return, or if the hot dry years of several thousand years ago repeat themselves, our lives must change. We must adapt.

The geologic story of Longs Peak starts so long ago that the reality of its connection to our own lives sometimes flickers and dims. But the story continues. And these days it rafts us along like the brittle surface ice of a glacier, ready to send crevasses through our complacency, surge us downstream into a well-watered future, or strand us on a drying plain.

On a fulcrum of rock this mountain balances a past challenging to decipher and a future difficult to imagine. And all the while, water streams from its summit to its base, shaping and nourishing Longs Peak, bringing its present to life.

AT each moment, the mountain is alive with the comings and goings of creatures, its forests and meadows humming with courtship and play, feeding and death. A pika pauses at the top of a boulder on the shore of Chasm Lake, headed for its winter haypile with a spray of alpine avens blossoms clenched firmly in its teeth.

At the same moment a white-breasted nuthatch flits to a ponderosa pine in Wild Basin, working its way up the fragrant trunk in search of insects. In a spruce along Boulder Brook, a goshawk perches attentively—ready to launch at the first sign of movement from a junco or blue grouse caught unaware.

Each Longs Peak creature has distinct tolerances for elevation, moisture, temperature, and exposure to storms. Plants and animals with similar needs have evolved in unique communities, yet each must cope with a mountain climate that can change within a few feet, making survival easy or impossible.

THE ROARING, STORMING FRONT RANGE WIND. Longs Peak

is the northernmost 14,000-foot summit in the Rocky Mountains. The Continental Divide reaches farther east in the Front Range than anywhere else in North America. From the mountain—just east of the Divide—the earth drops 9,000 feet to the Great Plains in twenty miles.

Winds consequently play around this mountain of extremes in remarkable ways. Winter gusts on the summit have been clocked at 201 miles per hour, ranking Longs Peak as one of the world's windier places (along with Mount Washington, New Hampshire; Mount Fuji, Japan; Antarctica; and Greenland). *Chinooks*, warm winds following the westerlies downslope, have raised temperatures on the plains thirty degrees Fahrenheit in three minutes.

Most winter storms blow in from the west; maximum winds owe their severity to the jet stream dipping close to Front Range summits. Upslope storms come in spring—carrying Gulf air from the southeast,

Ponderosa pines ring the base of the peak, a fringe of great trees distinctive with long, pungent needles, spine-tipped globular cones, and orange-plated bark.

with considerable oceanic moisture. They generally do not reach into the mountains past 9,000 feet, but they shower foothills forests with maximum moisture for the year, perfectly timed for the growing season.

Spring storms can be spectacular indeed. In April, 1921, 76 inches of snow fell in 24 hours at 10,400-foot Silver Lake (about fifteen miles south of Longs Peak). When the storm ended after 30 hours, 90 inches of snow blanketed the frozen lake. This remains the national record for a 24-hour snow.

In summer, warming air rises, cools, and with sufficient moisture, condenses into spectacular afternoon thunderheads. Lightning has claimed lives on Longs Peak. Summit-bound hikers must take great care in July and August, starting before dawn to insure descent by early afternoon.

Walking up the trail near treeline, the hard early morning sky vibrates with the intensity of its blue. Clouds surely could never mar its clear sweep of color. But a few panting steps later, when you look up from your boots to the horizon, a puff of white magically floats against the blue. Another switchback and the puff has companions. Each time you glance up, the clouds have grown, their tops graying—like a time-lapse, freeze-framed movie. Thunder rumbles over the Divide. The first flash of lightning seems like a blink—a pulse through your retina from a heart pumping in low gear. The second bolt can't be mistaken: ozone burns in the air. Time to head down the mountain.

Annual precipitation totals just 16 inches at Estes Park—directly in the rain shadow of the Divide and barely wetter than the plains. The Longs Peak massif begins near 8,500 feet, where perhaps 20 inches of moisture arrive yearly. At 10,000 feet, 30 inches accumulate—and the pattern of its arrival changes. Here, in the subalpine forest, and above, in the tundra, most of the year's moisture comes as winter snow; upslope spring storms usually do not reach this high. The highest tundra ridges may receive 40 inches or more of annual precipitation.

Front Range winds roaring over the Divide wreak havoc with this liberal total. They sweep most of the snow off the tundra and into subalpine forest, where it piles in deep drifts. Many areas above treeline remain blown free of snow all winter. Topography along the Divide funnels windblown snow into cirques where it nourishes the tiny existing glaciers—alive only at the behest of such winds.

The mountain endures lower temperatures and receives more moisture than a simple continental climate would predict. But minimum temperatures on the highest ridges usually reach no lower than basins and plains far below, for cold air pools in valleys at night. In traveling from plains to tundra on a January night, temperatures drop only about one degree Fahrenheit with each 1,000 foot rise. On a July day, however, temperatures lower almost five degrees with each climb upward of 1,000 feet. Subalpine forests again win the prize for moderation, catching

most of the snow, tempering the winds, experiencing the narrowest range of temperatures.

Whatever vegetation we might map today reflects only the *current* Front Range climate. In Pinedale time, glaciers filled valleys where today aspen and alder grow along streams. Precipitation exceeded modern totals by six inches annually, and average July days were cooler by nine degrees Fahrenheit. Tundra reached 1,600 feet lower. Swamps dotted the plains.

Like every other "sphere" of Longs Peak's world, the atmosphere and its climate bring constant change. Today is not like yesterday. Tomorrow will be different still.

FOOTHILLS FOREST: THE LAST PONDEROSA.

Longs Peak rises in a massif bounded by the great glacial valleys of North St. Vrain Creek, Glacier Gorge, and Glacier Basin on the south, west, and north respectively. On the east the peak drops to Tahosa Valley. The Twin Sisters separate the mountain from a smooth descent to the plains.

The west ridges merge with high country along the Continental Divide. On its other three sides, Longs Peak begins where Front Range foothills end, at 8,500 feet. The lowest point truly part of "the mountain" is the North St. Vrain Creek crossing at the mouth of Wild Basin, at 8,300 feet.

Ecologically, this is remarkably tidy. Foothills forest barely reaches Longs Peak. Above, the mountain is thoroughly subalpine and alpine.

All the way up from the plains, two foothills trees cloak the Front Range: ponderosa pine and Douglas-fir. They lightly fringe the base of the mountain, but few grow above 9,000 feet. Ponderosas favor dry, south-facing, rocky slopes. Douglas-fir needs more water; it shades north-facing slopes and ravines and grows in open country if sufficiently cool and moist.

Every ponderosa remains distinctive in a way that close-ranked lodgepole pine or fir can never feel. In her sensitive interpretation of Front Range foothills ecology, *Beyond the Aspen Grove,* Ann Zwinger described the distinctive odor of the pine.

> It is an evocative smell of cleanness and fresh air. It is neither sweet nor cloying. It does not assault the senses. It is straightforward and clear, changing with damp or dry weather, but always retaining its essential clarity and identity. It is unmistakable, just as the conifer itself can be confused with no other tree.

Ponderosas spread their roots wide to enable survival in dry soils.

**BEAVER
AND
ASPEN**

Snow lingers along Glacier Creek in early May. But between storms, the spring sun feels warmer each day. The iced-over beaver ponds above the confluence with Boulder Brook begin to glisten with a brilliant slick of meltwater.

Sunrise. Beneath the ice, the male beaver finally can see light begin to pierce his black winter world. Along the edge of the pond he shoves his bulky shoulders through a last frozen skin of ice and takes a deep breath of air thick with the heady smells of spring. He submerges and swims around the perimeter of the pond,

Mature trees stand apart from one another, and thus allow a good look at themselves: bark deeply furrowed and peeling off in orange-brown plates, open crowns, each springy twig bearing its rounded fistful of long needles.

Open ponderosa forests allow for grass and shrubby under-growth—dominated by bitterbrush and wax currant and favored by mule deer and elk as winter range. Abert's squirrels live only in ponderosa forests, where they feed on the pine's seeds and the tender inner cambium of new twigs. Birds—including the elegant pygmy nuthatch, Steller's jay, and western tanager—find abundant food and nesting sites in ponderosas. In winter, chickadees, nuthatches, juncos, kinglets, sparrows, and woodpeckers flock in multi-species bands.

This bright and open foothills forest world gives way quickly. A last few ponderosas stand in the meadows of Tahosa Valley and the checking for open water in other places. The beaver paddles leisurely, kicking with powerful webbed hind feet. This is a short swim: he can stay under water for fifteen minutes when necessary.

Two other places have melted out. Five months of winter darkness have ended. He returns to the lodge. Here the colony has spent the winter under the ice, he and his mate, three kits from the previous summer's litter, and two yearlings. They have lived off the tangle of aspen and willow they anchored with mud at the bottom of the pond last autumn.

Their dam and lodge, thoroughly repaired and replastered before winter, have been frozen for months—frozen as solid as Longs Peak granite. No predator can claw through the icy lodge. The rock-hard dam helps prevent their pond from draining low enough to freeze the entrance to the lodge, trapping them inside.

Late May. Preparing for birth, the pregnant female beaver shoos the others from the main lodge. The old male moves to a small emergency refuge along the bank. Last year's young beavers find other temporary dens. But the adults drive the two-year olds away from the pond. The parents bristle and snap, as stubbornly fixed on their goal as when they gnaw down a good-sized aspen.

Each of the two young beavers finally submits, instinctively intent on searching out a mate—and a homestead to build on—by autumn. One—the male—swims down Glacier Creek, barely out of sight of his home colony. The other outcast, a female, wanders farther, lumbering up Boulder Brook. She follows the dancing creek through aspen groves white-trunked against a blue sky, each twig tipped with promise: buds opening to green leaves. A good omen.

glades of lower Wild Basin. Douglas-fir mixes with spruce and lodgepole pine still farther up the peak. Gradually, lodgepoles and then spruce and fir take over.

Creeks tie together all these forests. Aspen and alder-lined, they run through the various sets of conifers, blithely and abundantly wet.

OUZELS, ALDERS, and FIRE PINES.

Throughout much of the West, water means cottonwoods. Longs Peak streams are no exception, lined with narrow-leaved cottonwoods on the lowest reaches of the mountain. Balsam poplar, alder, river birch, willow, aspen, and blue spruce accompany the cottonwoods. But with increasing elevation—and cold—the

Sandwiched between forests ruled by wind, cold, and drought lie the mountain's fire forests of lodgepole pine and aspen. Fire burns off stagnant lodgepoles; sun-loving fireweed blossoms under their charred trunks.

ranks of subalpine fir and Engelmann spruce close in. Distinctive riverbank forests peter out above 8,500-9,000 feet.

Even higher on the mountain, the singing rush of the creeks still attracts water-loving animals. Water ouzels—John Muir's favorite birds—haunt rapids, walking nonchalantly underwater along the stream bottom in search of insect prey. The mountain's only reptile, the wandering garter snake, favors marshy meadows, as do shrews and western jumping mice. Boreal toads and cricket frogs breed in ponds all the way to treeline.

Beaver long have been associated with Longs Peak. In nearly every one of his books, Enos Mills wrote of the big rodents (North America's largest), including one entire volume: *In Beaver World*. Most of his observations came from colonies around Longs Peak, including the Moraine Colony on lower Roaring Fork which Mills studied for 36 years.

Biologists again studied Mills's colonies in 1922 and 1955. With recent observations, we have a remarkable century-long record for these beaver ponds. Today, their populations have dropped, and ponds have drained or silted in, fated to become meadows and then forests.

Beaver activity along Roaring Fork has decreased as the rodents have eaten the aspen and willows. Roaring Fork beaver have felled lodgepole pine, but they do not enjoy it as a steady diet—or presumably they would have stayed. Along Glacier Creek just above Glacier Basin lie the most active ponds on the mountain, still flooded, still attracting their share of mink, muskrat, and waterfowl.

Perhaps our fascination with beavers lies in our shared ability to transform the land. We also share that ability with fire.

When pioneers moved into the mountains in the late 1800s, fires increased enormously in frequency. On the heels of huge, devastating wildfires came our more recent dedication to preventing them. Longs Peak forests have lost whatever balance they once had. Humans dictate today's fire regime.

Open ponderosa pine forest can survive frequent light fires. Above about 10,500 feet, spruce and fir very slowly replace mature subalpine forest lost in a burn. But at mid-elevations, fire triggers a complex series of events. Here, aspen and lodgepole pine, the opportunists of the Longs Peak forests, find their place.

Both trees have adapted beautifully to fire. Lodgepole is a relentless specialist that can do only one thing well, but it does that one thing better than any other tree. The mountain stands knee deep in lodgepole pines. They banish aspen, a flamboyant eccentric, to marginal environments.

Tightly closed lodgepole cones remain on the tree for years until the hot blaze of a forest fire roasts them open and melts resin encasing the seeds. The popping cones spray fresh ashes with lodgepoles-to-be.

CHICKAREE AND MARTEN

The squirrel awoke. Pastel light filled Wild Basin as the earth spun eastward and the sun neared the rim of the plains. Time to go to work.

This female chickaree had four young, weaned just a month ago and getting so big now in August that the nest could scarcely hold them. As she left the nest for a perch along the spruce branch to groom her rich brown fur, the mother jostled her young awake. The five squirrels ran down the great trunk, claws scratching furrowed spruce bark.

They dashed only a few feet before the adult stopped on a downed lodgepole. She listened; she tested the still air for scent. Nothing came her way but the soft, wet smell of the meadow at

Aspen, on the other hand, reproduces mostly by sprouting from roots, shooting up new trunks in profusion after fire.

Both trees do best on sunny, open slopes. But as they grow and mature, they doom themselves by protecting seedlings of the shade-tolerant species which gradually overtop them: Douglas-fir at lower elevations and subalpine fir and Engelmann spruce above.

From about 9,000 to 10,000 feet on the mountain, lodgepole does not often give way to other conifers. Fire deserves credit, burning off stagnant forest, allowing trees to start fresh. Evidently these stable lodgepole forests grow on sites too cold for Douglas-fir and too dry for subalpine trees.

Mountain pine beetles also can prolong the life of lodgepole stands, thinning the forest by killing mature trees, keeping the stand productive.

Sandbeach Lake, floating over a constant background chorus of sharply pungent spruce and fir.

The squirrels moved farther, two hundred feet from the nest, with several sudden stops for danger checks. They reached a clump of large Engelmann spruce and ascended, radiating onto separate branches like Blue Angel jets peeling off at the top of a climb. Each chickaree began work on its branch, biting off a cone every few seconds. Spruce cones rained down on the forest floor in syncopated plops.

Suddenly the female set up a frantic chatter. The young squirrels joined in; so did a Steller's jay, for good measure. A male chickaree was passing by on the edge of the grove. He called to the female, using the "password," asking permission to trespass peacefully. She chattered back, but did not give chase. He moved on.

The squirrel family descended to gather their harvest: eighty-three spruce cones in just a few minutes. Now began the relay to the midden, the squirrels thrusting each cone deep beneath the litter of scales and gnawed cone cores left in a swale by generations of chickarees.

Peace abruptly turned to chaos. A marten sprang from out of nowhere—so it seemed to the chickarees—pinning the sole young male to the root of a spruce, and killing it with a bite to the base of its skull. No squirrel ever ran faster than the others, too alarmed even to scold.

The marten, its pelt brown as the earth, took the limp squirrel in its mouth. With a glance at the escaping survivors that embodied the skill, stealth, and dignity of a master hunter, it headed for cover, intent on eating its first meal in a day—hair, bones, and all.

As spruce and fir overtake lodgepoles, however, pine beetles deplete the stands of pine and hasten them toward their destiny.

Aspen do best at the edges of meadows and along streams. Large aspen trees grow in Wild Basin, and substantial groves fringe Glacier Creek's beaver meadows. These glades have deeper, wetter soils than coniferous stands, more soil invertebrates, and lush understories. But don't expect a blaze of fall color across the slopes of Longs Peak. Lodgepole pine outcompetes aspen in these fire forests. Most of the mountain's mid-elevations are dry-floored, dark, and nearly sterile stands of fire pines.

Few forests show less variety. Chickarees (pine squirrels) find the lodgepoles beneficent, covered with dependable cones year-round. Not many other mammals would agree.

Bierstadt Lake reflects Longs Peak
and a colonnade of spired subalpine
fir and Engelmann spruce. Between
the dark conifers red-berried
kinnikinnick carpets the ground. On
a rocky ridge nearby, a gray jay
perches in a pine.

L ONGS PEAK, YUKON TERRITORY.

On all but the driest of sites between about 10,000 feet and treeline, subalpine fir and Engelmann spruce dominate the mountain. They form a forest called subalpine or boreal, the latter because increasing elevation mimics an increase in latitude: spruce-fir forests on Longs Peak strongly resemble the boreal spruce-fir forest of northern Canada.

Big predators hunted the subalpine forest (before we hunted and harrassed them to local extinction): lynx, wolverine, grizzly, and wolf. Red-backed voles still live under windthrown logs, and gray jays fly through blizzards. Chickarees scold nearly everything that moves.

From Canada to Longs Peak, the Rocky Mountain spruce-fir forest remains remarkably similar (some say monotonous). But like every living community on Longs Peak, subalpine forest has its nuances. It spans a wide range of environments from boggy to dry. It grows in cool, sheltered valleys at the base of the peak, and at treeline where it creeps out to interfinger with the tundra.

The biggest trees grow on wetter ground. Such moist spots usually escape fires, and their sheltered nooks prevent frequent blowdowns. Ecologist Beatrice Willard described the lush forest of Wild Basin as *still* wild, with spruce, fir, and aspen of "exceptional size and perfection of form."

Across the spectrum of available moisture, blueberry varieties carpet the forest floor. Myrtleleaf blueberry gives way to broom huckleberry in higher, drier stands. The shiny acid-green leaves of both serve as counterpoint to the dark greens of the mature conifers and the pale creamy-green of new spruce growth. Here and there rises a clump of yellow-blossomed heart-leaved arnica, or little heath-like pyrolas. In sunny meadows along streams grow dense patches of arrowleaf ragwort and tall mertensia.

Dominance is a tricky concept. By several measures, Engelmann spruce dominates the forest. It grows larger, lives longer (450 versus 300 years), and covers more area than subalpine fir. Root-rotting fungi pose a problem to adult firs, weakening the trees, which the wind then can fell more easily. Fir, however, reproduces more successfully and occurs in higher numbers than spruce.

Perhaps this all sums up to co-dominance. Both trees give the subalpine forest its feel. Graceful spires of subalpine fir look more like Christmas trees than any other conifer. Their cones, purple when young, stand upright like decorative candles. Spruce seem rough-hewn by comparison, with needles four-sided instead of flat, more spreading spires, drooping cones, and darker demeanor.

On the driest ridges, on the shallowest, coarsest soils, and where

CLARK'S NUTCRACKER AND LIMBER PINE

One calm and crisp September day, the nutcracker set a record: it cached 938 limber pine seeds. With its flock, it worked through the windblown trees called Goblin's Forest along East Longs Peak Trail. The cone crop seemed endless, and the energy of the nutcrackers placed the only limit on the seed harvest.

The nutcracker moved among the stout pines, inserting its tapered bill between the cone scales and efficiently plucking each seed from its core. The jay transported the seeds in a pouch under its tongue, carrying more than one hundred seeds at once. On this trip, it left the grove when it had 88 seeds.

With a succinct "craw," the nutcracker flapped up toward the summit of Battle Mountain. Its calls came in raucous counterpoint to the smooth rhythm of its wingbeat.

the wind howls most constantly, spruce and fir give way to limber pine. On Longs Peak—and throughout the northern Front Range—limber pine differs from the rest of the Rockies. Elsewhere, it grows low on the mountains. South of James Peak near Berthoud Pass, bristlecone pine takes over at the highest, driest sites; in the Northern Rockies, whitebark pine fills this role. But in the absence of these two species, as on Longs Peak, limber pine grows on dry, rocky sites from below 7,000 feet in the foothills to treeline at 11,500 feet.

Not many other plants survive on these ridges with the tough pine. Dwarf juniper and kinnikinnick grow on the dry soils, and with a bit of extra moisture, aspen joins the stand. Limber pine also can replace dry spruce-fir forests after fire, coexisting with the "nobler" conifers until they return to dominance. But on the driest outposts, it remains alone—alone with the wind and the Clark's nutcrackers.

The journey lasted only a few minutes, for the cache site lay just a few hundred feet above Goblin's Forest. This sunny—and windy—south slope of Pine Ridge remained snow-free through the winter. Here, the nutcracker landed at the base of an old pine and hopped across the rotting granite between its roots. It thrust its bill into the weathered rock, spread its jaws to make a hole, and dropped a few seeds into each cache.

Its pouch emptied, the nutcracker swooped up to the snagged top of the big pine and took a good look at its cache site, for it would find these stored seeds in winter by remembered landmarks.

It took off with a dashing swoop, and headed back for another pouchful of pine seeds. Distinct as its call, the jay's black and white wings beating over the blurred green of the forest traced a pattern as sharp as crisply-printed type on bright white paper. Before the nutcracker quit for the day, it made eleven trips from forest to ridge-top. Before the flock ended their harvest, they had cached half a ton of limber pine seeds.

Through the winter the jays returned to sunny places all over the east flanks of the mountain, digging up stored seeds. When nesting time came in the spring, they had a food supply already at hand.

A number of caches the nutcracker made on the day it set its record never were reclaimed. The following spring, a wet one, the seeds sprouted in the shelter of the old pine's roots where the jay had planted them. One would survive.

In a few years another generation of nutcrackers would find plenty of limber pines to feed from on Battle Mountain.

TAKING TREES TO THEIR LIMITS.

Between 11,000 and 11,500 feet, Longs Peak subalpine forests dwindle and disappear, giving way to alpine tundra. The last holdouts form a line of wind-contoured trees that have acquired character in their triumph over the elements. They grow on a human scale, spruce scaled down to shrub-size, like gnarled old men, firs not lofty but looking us straight in the eye.

Treeline across the northern hemisphere generally matches the limit of 50-degree Fahrenheit average summer temperatures. A growing season any colder slows decomposition crucial to soil formation and does not give trees a chance for sufficient respiration to renew needles or to add a slender new layer of wood. Thus trees on Longs Peak reach 11,500 feet, but in northern Montana, only 7,500 feet.

We can read the results of the wind in the shapes of treeline—gnarled elfin woodland and here and there a tough lone limber pine.

On a smaller scale, an assortment of challenges makes treeline a checkerboard where tree islands stand surrounded by meadows and strips of shrubby *krummholz* (German for "crooked wood") interfinger with tundra. Wind and snow patterns determine where trees will make it. In areas blown snow-free, winter winds drive ice crystals before them like a sand-blasting machine, drying and killing needles. Late-lying snow smothers needles and seedlings. With just the right balance of snow accumulation, winter snowpack protects conifers but melts soon enough in spring to irrigate seedlings and allow needles to take advantage of the growing season.

These powerful forces add up to one overriding criterion dictating chances for each tree's survival: moisture availability. Wind transforms the highest part of the mountain into an alpine desert. It dries out plants most severely in winter, when they cannot counter with water from soil that remains frozen for five months or more each year.

We can read the results in the shapes of the trees. At the uppermost limits, only low cushions of krummholz survive, protected by snow accumulation through winter gales. A bit lower, a few stems rise above the main mass of wind-pruned branches, each stem flagged by the wind, with only its leeward twigs surviving. Lower still, where islands of spruce grow in meadows, branches of solitary trees brush the ground and take root. Rings of young trees eventually surround each old central spruce.

Sprouting from branches forms the key to krummholz development. A seedling gets its start in a sheltered spot, and slowly grows into a rounded cushion of tangled twigs. When it risks branches above the windbreak, winter tempests beat it back. As windward twigs lose their needles, leeward branches send down new roots, adding a fresh layer to replace each dying one. This layering seems capable of keeping a single individual alive for thousands of years. Trees on Longs Peak thus may have germinated in quite different climates, surviving as relicts where spruce and fir seedlings cannot sprout and survive today.

Animals use these elfin woodlands for shelter and nesting sites. White-crowned sparrows call from the thickets. Golden-mantled ground squirrels and least chipmunks scamper through in summer. Ptarmigan (high-elevation grouse) shelter in them year-round.

Marmots live at every elevation on Longs Peak—wherever rockpiles lie near meadows. Most conspicuous in open tundra, they live near treeline in abundance. These rodents emerge from hibernation with the spring thaw in April or May, and breed within two weeks. After a month's gestation and a month in the burrow, soft-furred young marmots make their appearance on the mountain.

They join a treeline world savoring its brief summer. Meadows blossom through long sunny days; animals bear new generations. In

summer, the life of a marmot is enviable: mammalogist David Armstrong compares it to that of "tourists on well-earned vacation; marmots are gourmands and heliophiles, they eat and they sunbathe."

They also carefully maintain a dominance hierarchy, rework their burrow systems, and remain ever alert to warnings whistled to the colony, triggering a general dash down burrows to avoid danger. Marmots live highly social lives. They communicate with visual signals, a "greeting" that involves touch and smell, and a vocabulary of six whistles, a scream, and threatening "tooth chatter." Pikas pay attention to marmot warning whistles, and marmots react when pikas chirp to announce danger.

In autumn, marmots look even more indolent as they grow roly-poly with fat to sustain them through hibernation. Lower-elevation colonies hibernate earlier than higher ones, perhaps because the high country's late spring postpones peak succulence in vegetation.

Even high-elevation marmots retire into hibernation by October. Winter chill descends on forest, krummholz, and tundra alike. Few animals brave the Longs Peak winter directly, and fewer still brave it above the shelter of elfin woodland at treeline. Above lies the tundra, where no trees grow, an alpine world challenging to plants and wild creatures, and exhilarating—if a little threatening—to people.

"... none too wide a thoroughfare... unbanistered space before it."

Enos Mills, 1920.

THE ALPINE WORLD.

Think of Longs Peak as a stepped pyramid with three tiers. The broad base is a green skirt of forests; the two upper levels form the alpine world.

Uppermost is the summit block, beginning about 12,600 feet above the sea, at the head of the Boulder Field and at the base of the East Face. The gentler slopes of tundra meadows form the middle tier, bounded by an 11,500-foot treeline below and the great cliffs of the climber's mountain above. In this middle world, small plants and subtle transitions reflect the large, harsh facts of alpine climate.

More than any other factor, snow cover dictates the rules of survival to the tundra. Winter winds create a mosaic of near-permanent snowbanks separated by areas scoured bare of snow.

Both snow-accumulation areas and snow-free areas have their disadvantages. Plants overwintering under snowpatches gain protection from drying, freezing winter winds but they must submit to cold, short growing seasons. In areas blown free of snow, plants must survive extreme cold and wind through winter and improvise ways to obtain moisture during dry summers. But they also maximize the length of their growing season, with no need to wait for snowmelt to take full advantage of summer sun and warmth.

PTARMIGAN AND WILLOW

The morning was blindingly clear except for a strange, sharp-edged cloud that cut across the sky over the Diamond. Seven male ptarmigan moved through willows poking above the snow in Chasm Meadow. Pure white, their lushly-feathered feet made fine snowshoes.

The grouse worked through the willows, snipping off buds and twigs with their beaks. They had moved into the meadow in October, and now in January had seen half the winter pass. Their daily schedule was simple: stay warm, eat, get fat. Be ready for mating come spring. The males wintered close to spring breeding grounds. Female ptarmigan wintered in larger flocks in willows farther down the mountain.

Two tundra communities depend on abundant moisture: the *snowbed* itself, and *marshes* at the edges of tarns and along streams of meltwater. Two other communities survive only in snow-free areas: *fellfields* in rocky soils and *alpine turf* in the deep soil of meadows. Pocket gophers churn the ground to create a distinctive environment for a plant community of their own.

Snowbed communities remain stable from decade to decade. Concentric circles of plant communities ring melting snowbanks, each band toward the center adapted to a shorter growing season. The last plants to melt out enjoy a waterlogged summer of only three to eight weeks before snow begins to accumulate once more.

Where winds batter the Longs Peak tundra full force, little snow accumulates—even in mid-winter. Here, highly specialized cushion and

44

Moving to a new willow, one male walked with a slight limp. In a violent storm last summer, a well-aimed hailstone had broken his left leg. It healed smoothly, but that leg now was shorter than the other. He found it no problem, and was as plump as his flock-mates, week by week efficiently turning willow buds into body heat and ptarmigan fat.

A dark shape banked over the ridge, mirrored by a swift shadow passing across the snowy basin. The golden eagle dipped low. The ptarmigan froze. White on white gave no clues to the eagle. It flew on, hungry, and the flock returned to feeding after a time.

As the day progressed, the birds periodically rested in the lee of shrubby spruce and willow. The weather was changing. A cold front, announced by the slash of cloud over the peak, had grayed the sky. Huge plate-like snowflakes began to swirl down over the shoulders of the mountain, seeming to stream through the Notch and take aim for the meadow.

The storm was a big one. Winds plumed snow over the Divide and eastward past the summit of Longs Peak, sifting it into the head of Roaring Fork in bursts of fine crystals. The ptarmigan fed through part of the afternoon, but the wind and snow ended their day early. Each chose its time, burrowing into soft drifts behind granite boulders for the night.

The limping male favored a bank of snow shielded by a house-sized rock. He scraped a hollow with his claws, nosed in, and wriggled deeper. A white puff of feathers, he disappeared into the powdery snow. Under the drift, he fluffed out his down, well-insulated by snow and feather from the gale above. He lay still. Fourteen hours until dawn.

mat plants invade rocky fellfields. Some fellfields remain fellfields. The wind wins, creating alpine deserts relieved only by the toughest cushion plants.

But fellfields are the most dynamic of Rocky Mountain tundra communities. Cushion plants slowly build soil and gradually can give way to sedge meadows—alpine turf. At any stage in the process, pocket gophers or voles may disturb the fragile cover over newly-formed soil and send plants off on a successional side track.

Over centuries, most snow-free areas develop toward the climax of Longs Peak tundra: the lush, resilient sod of sedge meadows diverse with wildflowers. Only catastrophic disturbance can disrupt this turf: human foot traffic, burrowing rodents, or a windstorm powerful enough to flip a crucial rock or chunk of turf and create a six-foot blowout.

In winter, Longs Peak turns white as the coat of an ermine. Snow plumes off the East Face and drifts in pockets on the tundra, in a great blanket within the subalpine forest.

THE THREE-WEEK SUMMER OF A SNOWBED.

Winter. Above ground, storms rage, winds blast. Temperatures plummet below zero. Under the snowbank, all is still. Ground temperature hovers around a stable 26 degrees Fahrenheit. Plants lie dormant, protected, safe.

Summer. Most of the tundra is in full flower. The snowbank melts a little more each day, exposing at its edge the rings of plants just beginning to break from winter dormancy. Glistening yellow snow buttercups open as they push away a last bit of the dirty white drift. White snowlover and the small rose sibbaldia blossom from cold, waterlogged soil.

Melting out first, arctic willow grows in depressions shallowly drifted over in winter. These Lilliputian shrubs make krummholz trees seem like giant redwoods. Ancient arctic willow twigs one or two inches long interfinger in ground-level thickets, catching windblown dust, building soil.

Also well-drained, but melting out later, tufted hairgrass forms the only true grass community of the Rocky Mountain tundra. On Longs Peak this grass grows in feathery tufts in wet snowbed communities but does not spread in luxuriant midsummer meadows as it does on Trail Ridge.

Next to melt out, Drummond's rush usually manages a growing season of 5 to 10 weeks in its waterlogged soil. It forms dark-green turf brightened by black-headed daisies (white on top, dark underneath). Risking no summer at all when snowfall is heavy, droopy tussocks of Pyrenees sedge emerge last from the snowbanks. Even in "normal" seasons, these sedges may see only three weeks of growth before fall comes.

Insects blown onto the surface of melting snowbanks make for rich foraging by flocks of brown-capped rosy finches. And meltwaters trickling down toward the six major streams of the mountain provide drinking water for tundra visitors from bull elk to hikers.

Along these streams, next to glacial tarns, and behind solifluction terrace dams, alpine marshes develop. Of all the alpine tundra communities, these are the most reminiscent of the arctic, with waterlogged soil, permafrost, and frost hummocks.

Here, willow shrubs form ideal summer nesting sites for white-crowned sparrows and wintering areas for ptarmigan. Marsh marigolds (in spring) and rose crown and Rocky Mountain lousewort (in summer) blossom along the streams. Coarse-leaved Rocky Mountain sedge grows from the mucky, peaty streamside soil, insulating saturated ground or permafrost beneath.

Creamy honey polemonium and purple sky pilot mark a gopher garden; yellow rydbergia always faces east to the dawn; and delicate purple-veined artic gentians bloom in late summer.

Distinctive rushes and sedges root in the gravel of frost scars that are flooded with even-temperature (frigid!) running water. Here too grows koenigia, a tiny buckwheat that is a tundra rarity, an annual plant—struggling to sprout, bloom, attract a pollinator, and set seed in the few weeks worth of growing season each fleeting tundra summer. Though it probably grows here since its companion species do, botanists have not yet spotted koenigia on Longs Peak.

THE UNCUSHY LIFE OF CUSHION PLANTS.

Two trails lead from treeline below Jims Grove to Granite Pass. One climbs the north-facing slope of Mills Moraine toward Chasm Lake Junction. The other passes through the last trees of Jims Grove and along the south-facing flank of Battle Mountain. In the basin between, late-lying snow outlines snowbed communities. Marshes ring still pools, their sedges a conspicuous emerald-green in fall when other tundra plants fade to tan and turn burnished gold and red.

But on the windblown trails, unwatered rock reigns. Fellfield cushion plants and alpine androsace pioneer the Battle Mountain side of the basin. Mountain dryad banks terraces on Mills Moraine. Both communities succeed to sedge meadows on flats where snow-free soil deepens to four inches.

On the south-facing slope, tundra plants show their most remarkable adaptations. Exposed here to the full brunt of alpine extremes, wind scours away protective soil and snow. It abrades plants, dries moist tissues, and disturbs the still "boundary layer" among plant stems. Temperatures fluctuate wildly. Gravelly soil drains rapidly.

Moss campion and alpine nailwort hug this ground, moderating the temperature with a thick cushion of shoots that traps soil and moisture. At first they grow quickly, at least quickly for an alpine plant; they spread across half an inch in five years, seven inches in twenty-five years.

Other fellfield plants have developed succulent leaves or flat rosettes. Most protect their leaves with hairs. They develop flower buds in late summer and protect them through winter to allow for quick flowering and maximum time for fruiting. Some buds may develop for four years.

On Longs Peak, the little annual alpine androsace plays an unusually dominant role in fellfields. Alpine clover forms dense mats that spread by taking root where its tiny branches touch the earth. In midsummer, rydbergia adds its great yellow blossoms to fellfield clover gardens. This spectacular alpine sunflower makes a fitting mascot for

Colorado columbine

48

Rydbergia stands above a miniature meadow of alpine clover.

the blazing sunlit world of dry Rocky Mountain tundra: it is closely related to desert plants.

Winds buffeting north-facing slopes blow not just dry and brutal, they blow cold and dry and brutal. Here, evergreen alpine dryad clings tenaciously to shaded rocky slopes at inclines up to 30 degrees. Solifluction and frost action move the rocky soil, but bands of tough dryad stabilize it, building turf. As scree moves downhill it carries the dryad with it, tilting the plants on end to form "risers" between bare flat steps. Dryad-banked terraces on Longs Peak would look familiar to Russian, Swiss, and Eskimo botanists; the plant is circumpolar.

PATH TO AN ALPINE MEADOW.

In favorable sites, with hundreds or thousands of years of chances, tall plants gain a foothold in the mass of dead shoots and soil built by old cushion plants. One ecologist tallied 93 pairs of invading erect plants and host cushions in the park. This invasion is the first step on the path to alpine turf.

Alpine forget-me-nots characterize a fellfield on its way to a meadow. Their mats, looser than the hardy nailwort and moss campion, bloom in masses of brilliant blue flowers. They match the most vivid blue of the sky over Longs Peak. A color should be named for them: alpine blue.

Both fellfields and dryad terraces may develop into full-fledged turf. Rock sedge dominates the open, rough transition meadows. Finally these too give way—with more centuries—to the lushest of tundra plant communities, the elk sedge meadow.

On Longs Peak, elk sedge (kobresia) meadows cover the whole middle tier of the mountain, except for slopes too steep, depressions too wet, and fellfields still too gravelly. They thrive only in the same snow-free areas as fellfields; late-lying snow kills them.

Kobresia indicates *real* soil, humus entangled in a mass of sedge roots that forms an incredibly efficient trap for summer thundershower runoff. A cubic foot of kobresia turf will absorb two to three gallons of water. In alpine meadows such soils may reach several feet in thickness, over a period of 400 to 1,300 years.

A huge number of other species (a fifth of them lichens) grows in these meadows—far exceeding any other alpine community in diversity. Water pipits and horned larks nest between sedge tussocks, exploding from underfoot when you step close. The wildflowers catch your eye until fall, when alpine avens turns red and kobresia a rich velvety gold—the dominant colors of the autumn tundra.

Most kobresia turf on Longs Peak has survived the tens of thousands of hikers. Only along trails and at heavily used spots like Jims Grove has it been destroyed. But given the centuries it takes to recover, biologists have called alpine turf "irreplaceable" and the National Park Service manages it as such.

After arctic climate and snow accumulation lay down their ultimatums, after some turf has been sacrificed to trail use, the primary factor varying the mosaic of meadows is, of all things, the pocket gopher.

GOPHER GARDENS *and* GRIZZLY BEARS.

Of the year-round mammal residents of the tundra, most hikers see only marmots and pikas; a few lucky ones spot a weasel. The abundant meadow voles, shrews, and mice remain invisible. But the pocket gopher leaves a telltale calling card that gives it away.

Throughout the tundra, fresh pocket gopher diggings break the smooth expanse of turf. The melting snowpack reveals tubelike burrow workings on the ground surface, showing where the gophers traveled under the snow during winter and then packed the resulting tunnels with soil from below ground. Dense gopher populations can move four to eight tons of topsoil per acre per year.

Where gophers turn up fresh soil, a characteristic group of plants invades, forming "gopher gardens." Skypilot, alpine avens, cinquefoils, greenleaf mertensia, and fernleaf candytuft take over in wetter sites; American bistort, arctic sage, and a group of grasses and sedges favor drier spots. These plants do grow elsewhere. Indeed, alpine avens is the most widespread flower in the Rocky Mountain tundra, with bistort a close second. But where they grow together in freshly exposed soil, gophers have been gardening.

These erect plants die out after several decades. Cushion plants invade, and a patch of fellfield mars the lush turf. Gophers may prolong the life of these disturbed areas, or they may succeed to kobresia turf within a few centuries.

Voles, too, can transform plant communities. They overwinter under shallow snow, where they normally eat grasses and sedges along their diminutive runways. When vole populations periodically skyrocket, they shred the centers of cushions, killing the plants, and set the stage for alpine avens to invade each remnant cushion. Years later, if you look closely around the roots of the avens, shredded bits of the vole-killed cushion give away its history.

Where boulderfields lie next to meadows, marmots and pikas make their homes. Unlike marmots, pikas do not hibernate. They begin stockpiling their winter haypile in mid-June, continuing until the first heavy snow. One pika may collect about 35 pounds of dry storage in a single season. With their high metabolism they must fill their stomach almost hourly.

Pika calls sound more metallic and burry than a marmot whistle. The pika vocabulary includes a territorial declaration, a set of dominance/submissiveness messages, and the familiar alarm call. Pikas signal danger when any bird larger than a robin flies over the colony. Weasels and martens stalk pikas, and coyotes eat juveniles.

With their cobble-sized gray bodies, pikas blend in with their rocky home. Watching one haying is irresistible—once you have spotted it. The alarm call can sound ear-splittingly close, while its proclaimer remains invisible. Too small to hunt for game or pelts, and living in a habitat "useless" to people, pikas still thrive. Unfortunately, the larger high mountain mammals have not fared as well.

Bison once grazed Longs Peak tundra in summer, along with elk and bighorn sheep. Elk, reintroduced in the park, have done well, though Longs Peak is not part of their important range.

Wolves, grizzly bears, wolverines, and lynx hunted through the Longs Peak forests. The last northern Colorado grizzly roamed 200 square miles of high country around Longs Peak—the "Echo Mountain" grizzly, a three-legged female with cubs. Enos Mills told her tale in his 1922 book *Watched by Wild Animals*. Today, these animals are gone from the mountain.

Longs Peak has lost life forms that thrived upon it for millenia. Ten thousand hikers a year have replaced grizzly, wolf, and bison. Most of them spend only a few hours here, perhaps a few days. None of them spend a lifetime. The mountain subtly shifts its weight, redistributes its populations, and finds a new balance.

In the late 1800s, Enos Mills knew a truly wild Longs Peak—when grizzlies, wolves, and bighorn sheep still ranged the mountain.

THE HIGHEST WORLD. Both alpine worlds—tundra meadows ringing the middle tier of the mountain and above them the highest cliffs—survive extremes of climate that exceed the tolerance of trees. Tundra plants begin to absorb nutrients and to grow as soon as temperatures rise above freezing; lowland species require a warm 40-50 degrees Fahrenheit.

On the uppermost tier, the rugged shape of the mountain overrules all other environmental factors. Only where cliffs relent and allow for a tiny pocket of soil can flowering plants grow. Crevices and ledges support a unique combination of alpine plants up to about 13,700 feet on these highest faces. Beyond, little but moss and lichen survives on the sheer walls.

The best examples of these ledge communities cling to the East

Alpine gardens require a close look. Between rounds of granite in the Boulder Field, alpine avens forms turf—and a staple food for rabbit-like pikas. Small pink whorls of rose crown grow along streams and feathery-tailed alpine dryad covers rocky terraces. Deep colors occur in tiny patches: glistening yellow snow buttercups, delicate blue columbines, and spectacular purple Parry primrose.

Yellow-bellied marmots live in rockpiles at every elevation on Longs Peak; along the trail through the tundra their warning whistles mark the passage of thousands of hikers each year.

Face. Walter Kiener, the climber and botanist who studied the Longs Peak tundra in exhaustive detail in the 1930s, described them: ". . . a pioneer community doing outpost duty on the climatic frontier of the realm of the flowering plants."

The great wall actually faces east-northeast, allowing only early morning sun to relieve the cold—as any East Face climber can testify. Watered by melting snow and ice, these window-box gardens of alpine flowers make do with an extremely short growing season. Tiny saxifrages dominate in numbers. Big-rooted springbeauty grows with them, its flat rosette of succulent leaves capturing maximum sunlight while staying low to the ground. A taproot up to six feet long and three inches in diameter anchors it to the wall and absorbs a full share of moisture.

As cliffs weather, boulders pile at their bases and tumble toward the meadows below. In such *talus*, another rockbound plant community develops, dominated by alpine thistle and its companions, a fern (appropriately named rockbrake) and a dwarf columbine. Pockets of soil on rock slopes provide considerable moisture, while boulders shelter plants from the wind. Tall Colorado columbine ventures high into the tundra in such habitats, delighting hikers surprised by it at 12,000-foot Granite Pass.

On the flat summit of Longs, a fugitive or two from lower elevations sometimes takes hold, softening the overwhelming bulk of rock. In his hundreds of Longs Peak climbs, Enos Mills recorded lichens, spike grass, sky pilot, primroses, phlox, and mertensia growing on top of the mountain.

As for animal visitors to the summit, Mills reported:

> . . . straggling bumblebees, grasshoppers, and at least two kinds of prettily-robed butterflies. Among the mammals visiting the summit I have seen a mountain lion, a bob-cat, a rabbit, and a silver fox, though only one of each. The bird callers include flocks of rosy finches, ptarmigan, and American pipits, numbers of white-crowned sparrows and juncos, together with a scattering of robins, bluebirds, golden eagles, red-tailed hawks, and humming birds!

In *The Adventures of a Nature Guide*, he added marmots, weasels, and bighorn sheep tracks to the "summit register," and identified the adventuresome rabbit as a cottontail.

Life on Longs Peak never gives in to the incredible challenges reeled off by the mountain. On the summit, where winds blow two hundred miles an hour in winter, robin and cottontail have visited in summer. On the Diamond, tiny gardens of saxifrage survive in spots inaccessible even to the gifted feet of rock climbers.

This mountain of rock is a mountain of life. Imperturbable and dynamic, both mountain and life prevail, the peak a rocky backdrop for the lives of beaver, jay, and primrose, and finally, for people.

53

chapter three

MOUNTAIN CHRONICLE

LONGS Peak history spans almost two billion years. The saga of its plants and animals began more than one billion years ago. Most familiar kinds evolved in the last 65 million years.

For most of us, none of this counts as much as the time since humans arrived on the scene. Human history—the "real" history of the mountain—includes only the last 15,000 years, and the earliest several thousands of those years are blank. In its narrowest definition—the written record—history has not yet tallied two centuries for Longs Peak. These last years give us most of our stories.

Our knowledge of the first North Americans amounts to little more than a few campsites and chipped stone tools. Understanding more of their lives is nearly impossible. These people remain the small figures in static museum dioramas, mammoth and bison hunters without names or personal history. We cannot hear them laugh and cry. We cannot feel their hearts lift when they look up to Longs Peak from a plains campfire.

We think of the days of Ute and Arapaho camps below the mountain as ancient and timeless. Yet the Arapaho did not reach Colorado until about 1800; their survivors left fifty years later, banished to reservations.

Beyond photographs and named heroes, beyond the time of our great-grandmother's grandfather, time goes fuzzy.

For thousands of years, history swirled around the mountain in a continuous daily log of unwritten events—loves, deaths, jokes, and hunts. Feel these times. Sight along your spear to the peak as you aim for a mammoth. Fast on Old Man Mountain and watch the rising sun gild the rock of Longs Peak. Race for the foothills with your family as the first winter storm rolls over the Divide and buries the rock walls of the clan's tundra game-drive with snow.

Longs Peak rising over the Indian-peopled plains—Samuel Seymour's rendition in the 1823 report of the Long expedition, first published depiction of the mountain.

After 1820, we can repeat "true" stories because people began to write down what they felt about the mountain. We even know the adventures of the last generation of Arapahoes here: we were able to ask them and record their answers.

Beyond the time of Stephen Long, Marcellus St. Vrain, Old Man Gun, and Rufus Sage, the history of Longs Peak is nameless. It always will remain a time of mystery and legend, no matter how many campsites we excavate, how many times we record the creation story of the Utes, or how insightfully we analyze the park potsherd collection.

The mountain has seen more stories than we can ever hear. The mountain always will know more than us.

GREAT PLAINS MAMMOTHS *and* ALPINE BISON.

12,000 B.C. On a steely gray day a band of new animals moved into Colorado. Above them, great peaks rose to the west, one summit higher than all the others, its valleys glacier-white, set off against deep colors of the rock.

These animals were like no other that had lived in North America. They built fires at night to warm themselves, they killed with stone points instead of fangs, and communicated with each other in complicated ways. They walked upright, looked at the world around them with curiosity and understanding, and though weak and slow, dominated every other creature.

They were humans, and North America would never again be the same.

We know of some of these people, the Paleoindians, from traces of their campfires and from the chipped projectile points that formed the crux of their livelihood. They hunted great game animals on the plains. Forty miles east of Longs Peak, a mammoth kill dating to 9250 B.C. has yielded their characteristic Clovis points. Similar points have turned up on Trail Ridge.

These hunters may have nudged to extinction the declining populations of large animals already having trouble coping with rapid changes in climate and vegetation. Giant deer, bison, and ground sloths; mammoths, horses, and camels—all disappeared soon after humans walked across the Bering land bridge and spread down the continent.

After the huge Pleistocene mammals disappeared—about ten thousand years ago—some hunting bands specialized on smaller bison, deer, or other game. Others took to foraging for plants and small animals. For thousands of years, cultures we class mostly by a single fragment of their lives—the shape of their projectile points—lived within sight of Longs Peak.

They moved with the game. And the game moved with the changing seasons and cycling climate. During persistent droughts on the plains from about 7,000 to 6,500 years ago, and again, from 6,000 to 5,500 years ago, the mountains gave refuge to people escaping prairie famine.

During these years, Indian bands lived at treeline in summer. High mountain plants gave variety to their diet: big-rooted springbeauty, alpine sorrel, limber pine seeds, blueberries. They hunted deer, elk, and bighorn sheep by driving them into ambushes, building low rock walls to turn them the desired direction. As many as thirty people worked together, funneling game upward from treeline to the hidden killers.

These people hunted on the mountain; one ancient projectile point from Longs Peak dates to between 8,000 and 6,000 years ago. High country geologist/archaeologist James Benedict has excavated campsites and mapped tens of kilometers of rock-walled game drives to the north and south, but no similar sites have turned up on Longs Peak—yet.

Springbeauty

Men and women who wandered across continents, who moved hundreds of miles with the migrating herds of game—these people investigated their land carefully. They needed easy passes, good summer hunting grounds, and sheltered wintering areas. Always they sought a better place to hunt, an edge on their neighbors that would get them through a drought or a hard winter.

We cannot know when the first tribal wanderer climbed the mountain. We will never know their identity or whether they climbed in search of visions, to catch eagles, or simply to see the view—for the sheer thrill of it. But it seems likely that several thousand years before pharoahs ruled Egypt or Sumerians built the first city in Mesopotamia, a hunter clad in skins stood on the summit of the mountain we call Longs Peak.

THE REVOLUTIONARY HORSE.

Little changed for thousands of years. About the beginning of the Christian Era, however, hunters of bison and small game began to learn a new lifeway. Agriculture reached the Colorado plains along rivers from the east. Pottery-making and the bow and arrow became known. Plains Indians lived in small villages near water up to about 1400 A.D., when a drought displaced them. Their sedentary life never resumed. Whichever Plains Indian first saw a Spanish horse made sure of that.

Most historic tribes whose names we recognize barely beat Spanish and French trappers to Longs Peak. Utes are the exception. Many experts—and the Utes themselves—believe their ancestors lived here

Ute warriors lived longest around Longs Peak, and horses helped them to hold the high country. Later came Arapahoes and Cheyenne.

10,000 years ago. Linguists, however, think they moved into the Colorado mountains from the west just three or four hundred years ago.

Either way, the Utes and their allies the Shoshones in northernmost Colorado held the high country against all comers. But the plains saw wave after wave of peoples moving south in great migrations, particularly after woodland tribes in the Midwest were displaced westward by pioneers with itchy feet in the young United States.

First came the Apaches, who controlled the plains by 1500. Two hundred years later, the Comanches, in alliance with the Utes, drove plains Apaches southward. In the late 1700s, Kiowas pushed through, battled with the Comanches for a time, then made peace and jointly occupied the land below the mountain. Finally, in the early 1800s, Arapaho and Cheyenne displaced the Comanches and Kiowas.

When native peoples acquired the horse from the Spanish in the mid-1600s, easier buffalo hunting and long-distance raiding revolutionized their lives, simplifying old problems, creating new ones. Mounted plains tribes roamed vast territories across the ocean of grass, following the bison herds. Ute horsemen ventured out from their mountain stronghold to hunt and raid on the plains.

When Colorado entered the realm of written history, Longs Peak lay on the frontier between mountain Utes and plains Arapaho. The time of glory for the mounted warriors was brief, but glorious indeed.

OLD MAN GUN'S EAGLE TRAP.

The tide of change came with the discovery of gold in Colorado in 1859. Arapahoes hunted where townspeople wanted to live, and by the 1870s, both the Arapaho and the buffalo disappeared from Colorado. The tribe was forced onto the Wind River Reservation in Wyoming, the bison slaughtered. Arapahoes last summered around Longs Peak in the 1860s.

Utes, still at peace, spent more time on the plains once the U.S. Army defeated their Arapaho enemies. By the 1880s they too were pushed from their mountains in a losing battle that ended on reservations in Utah and in the far southwest corner of Colorado.

Though Utes lived around Longs Peak the longest, we know most about the Arapaho vision of the mountain. For in 1914, the Colorado Mountain Club arranged for two elderly Arapahoes to return to Estes Park and tell their stories of living in this place as young men in the 1860s.

It was the last chance to do such a thing: Sherman Sage was 63 at the time, Gun Griswold, 73. A young bilingual Arapaho interpreted for their white companions Shep Husted and Oliver Toll. On a two-week

pack trip through the mountains, the two Arapaho men gave traditional names for most park features, many of them retained today. How many of their stories were true and how many truly *stories*—playful inventions for their gullible listeners—we will never know.

They spoke of battles and camps and adventures below Longs Peak, of fasting on the summit of "Sitting Man"—Old Man Mountain at the west edge of Estes Park. A main trail threaded Wind River Pass and Tahosa Valley—called "Where the Woman was Killed," for the time a party of Arapahoes rode under a dead tree at the pass and knocked loose the snag, which fell and killed a woman. The great rounded hollow of the Boulder Field was "The Rawhide Dish." Longs Peak and Mount Meeker were the "Two Guides," *nesotaieux,* double-summited landmark of the whole region.

Gun Griswold's father was Old Man Gun, one of the greatest of Arapahoes. A noted medicine man, hunter, trapper, and warrior, Old Man Gun used an herb known only to him that had the power to give fits to his enemies and subdue eagles and wild horses. He caught his bald eagles—for making feather headdresses—on the summit of Longs Peak.

Old Man Gun's eagle trap, according to his son, was "right up on top" of the mountain:

> . . . there is a hole dug in an oval shape. The top of it is big enough for a man to get down through, but it widens out below and is big enough for him to sit in. This was up there when he captured all those eagles, for it was an eagle trap. He had a stuffed coyote up there and some tallow. Gun used to sit in this hole so that he couldn't be seen, and put the coyote on the ground above him and the tallow by it. The eagles would see the coyote from a great distance, and would come to get it. When the eagles lit by the coyote, Old Man Gun would grab the eagles by the feet, reaching up by the back of the coyote.

When Old Man Gun touched an eagle with his herb-covered hands, the eagle "had a fit" and became helpless. He then twisted a cord around its feet to hold it. Gun would climb the mountain at night, when eagles could not see him. He chose the top of Longs Peak so the great birds would have no chance to light on trees, watching their fellows be caught, and catch on to Old Man Gun's tricks.

In 1859, Gun Griswold and five other young Arapahoes climbed up to see the trap ". . . because we had heard about it so much, just like you people go to see things." Even then, it was filling in, though the dirt that Old Man Gun dug from the hole "was scattered all over the mountain, as if a gopher had scattered it." The group climbed the peak from Wild Basin, probably by the same route used by John Wesley Powell ten years later; the rocks wore out their moccasins so fast, they had to put on a new pair every three hours. The Powell party saw no trace of the trap: frost action would not let such diggings last long.

Old Man Gun gives us a clue to the easy relationship tribal people had with the mountain. But most of its tragedies have been forgotten. Most of its triumphant climbs went unrecorded. This is all we know of the Native American history of Longs Peak.

MOUNTAINS INDEED.

Before the "discovery" of Longs Peak in 1820, Indians climbed the mountain numerous times. Spanish and French traders had wandered the Colorado plains for a couple of centuries, though no "official" Spanish explorations passed Longs Peak. French trappers named the mountain and neighboring Mount Meeker *Les Deux Oreilles*, the Two Ears.

American mountain men had taken beaver in the Colorado mountains at least since James Purcell in 1802. Ezekiel Williams trapped through Middle Park in 1811. By the time Major Stephen Long came calling in 1820, mapmaking equipment in hand, he could hire old hands like Joseph Bijeau to guide him. In the 1840s, "Pathfinder" John Charles Fremont had mountain men at his disposal—twenty-year veterans of the West who carried detailed atlases of the West mapped in their heads.

When Lieutenant Zebulon Pike made his abortive attempt to climb Pikes Peak in 1806, the great mountain close at hand preoccupied him. Pike did no rhapsodizing on distant views to the north.

After the War of 1812, the U.S. Army sent Major Stephen Long to scare off British traders in the mountains. Diverted to the Rockies from his original goal of the upper Missouri country in Montana, Long and his twenty-two men came within sight of the Front Range on June 30, 1820. After the long prairie march, expedition scientist Edwin James wrote of the close look it took to verify their hopes:

> For some time we were unable to decide whether what we saw were mountains, or banks of cumulous clouds skirting the horizon, and glittering in the reflected rays of the sun. It was only by watching the bright parts, and observing that their form and position remained unaltered, that we were able to satisfy ourselves they were indeed mountains.
>
> . . . Towards evening the air became more clear, and our view of the mountains was more satisfactory, though as yet we could only distinguish their grand outline, imprinted in bold indentations upon the luminous margin of the sky. We soon remarked a particular part of the range divided into three conic summits, each apparently of nearly equal altitude. This we concluded to be the point designated by Pike as the highest peak.

To everyone else, Longs Peak looks twin-summited from the plains.

60

Stephen Long came within forty miles of the mountain in 1820 and described its twin-summitted silhouette from the plains. His name remained behind, permanently linked with the peak.

However, Long and his companions did eventually correct their other initial miscalculation: as they marched south, Long sighted Pike's "highest peak" and James climbed it a few days later.

The first-spotted high peak remained unclimbed by the explorers, who approached no closer to it than forty miles. In the years to follow, trappers nonetheless began to call the mountain after its first chronicler: Longs Peak.

THE LAST MOUNTAIN MAN.

Through the 1820s and '30s many mountain men must have trapped the streams flowing from the mountain toward the plains. Mexico's independence from Spain in 1821 triggered the great Santa Fe trade, and the Colorado Rockies saw more beaver trappers than ever before. General William Ashley noted Longs from the Cache la Poudre River when he crossed the Front Range north of the peak in 1825. James Ohio Pattie mentioned seeing the mountain in 1826.

Late in the 1830s fur trade rivalries focused within sight of Longs Peak when a stubbornly independent Lancaster Lupton built Fort Lupton on the South Platte near its confluence with St. Vrain Creek. He opened for business midway between the trading empires commanded by the American Fur Company at Fort Laramie, Wyoming, and the Bents and St. Vrains at Bent's Fort to the south.

"The Company" retaliated with *two* competing forts, Jackson and Vasquez, run by old-timers Peter Sarpy, Henry Fraeb, and Louis Vasquez. The Bents and Ceran St. Vrain installed Ceran's young brother Marcellus at another new trading center—establishing four forts within a radius of fifteen miles.

Each of these small, lonely castles of timber and adobe saw their share of stories within the next decade. Fremont described Longs Peak from Fort St. Vrain in 1842, saying he ". . . was pleased to find that among the traders and voyageurs the name of 'Long's peak' had been adopted and become familiar in the country." The next year, Fremont celebrated the Fourth of July at the fort, eating ice cream that Marcellus St. Vrain claimed was made from Longs Peak snow. Francis Parkman came through in 1845, describing a stormy Longs Peak in his classic *The Oregon Trail*.

But the only traveler who wrote of going closer to the mountain was Rufus Sage. More tourist than trapper, Connecticut Yankee Sage wandered widely in the West from 1841 to 1843, spending considerable time at Fort Lupton. His 1846 book *Rocky Mountain Life* told of a month-long hunting trip to "the base of Long's Peak."

Sage described vegetation, geology, and the "numerous and varied attractions" of the region. His haunts seem to have included Estes and

In the 1830s and 1840s, posts like Fort St. Vrain on the South Platte River became resting and resupply points for trappers and travelers. Journal-keepers among them described the view of Longs Peak from the little fort.

Moraine parks, Marys Lake, and Wild Basin, "hemmed in upon the west by vast piles of mountains climbing beyond the clouds." His prose glowed purple:

> . . . occasional openings, like gateways, pointed to the far-spreading domains of silence and loneliness. . . . What a charming retreat for some one of the world-hating *literati*! He might here hold daily converse with himself, Nature, and his God, far removed from the annoyance of man.

Silk began to replace beaver as the stylish hat in the 1830s, spelling the doom of the beaver men. The last South Platte trading post, Fort St. Vrain, hung on until 1848. But the time of the mountain man ended in 1842, when Jim Bridger settled down in Wyoming to sell supplies to wagon trains. Kit Carson and Old Bill Williams took to guiding for Fremont. Tom Fitzpatrick and Jim Clyman began babying overland immigrants to Oregon and California.

The mountain had entered a new era.

LIVING WITH THE MOUNTAIN.

By the end of the 1840s, the Mexican War and the California Gold Rush transformed the West from the mountain man's wilderness domain to the promised land for settler and miner. Strikes in Colorado during 1858-1859 sparked the gold rush to Idaho Springs and Central City. Practically overnight, the mountain evolved from a barely-known legend to backyard landmark.

In 1859, Joel Estes, on the prowl for good land, worked his way through the foothills and found the great meadow that came to be called Estes Park. He brought his family to the park in 1860 and settled in, running cattle on the lush range, hunting the seemingly endless herds of elk, bighorn, deer, and pronghorn, marketing meat and skins in Denver.

Others followed on Estes's heels. The prospector Alonzo Allen built a cabin southeast of Longs Peak in 1864, finding disappointingly little gold, but lending his name to another forest meadow, Allens Park.

Meanwhile, Joel Estes and his family tired of the struggle against Front Range winters. They sold out in 1866, and their claim passed through several hands to come to rest with Griff Evans. This genial Welshman carried on the subsistence ranching and hunting of Joel Estes—and offered rough shelter and meals to the few adventurous tourists who began to visit the valley.

One of the first was William N. Byers, founder and editor of Denver's *Rocky Mountain News* and energetic promoter of the wonders of Colorado. Byers arrived in 1864, when the Estes family still held

John Wesley Powell tried to climb Longs Peak via this difficult arete leading from McHenrys Peak. Turned back, he finally reached the top from Wild Basin on August 23, 1868.

sway, and he named their homestead: Estes Park. He came with dreams to make the "first" climb of Longs Peak.

With his companions, Byers searched for a workable route to the summit from the Boulder Field, but gave up to try from the southeast. Byers and a Mr. Velie reached the summit of as yet unnamed Mount Meeker, adding their names "to the five registered before" (whose identities remain unknown). Disappointed, they failed to reach Longs itself, "upon which it looked as though a man must be tied to remain, if ever by any miracle he could reach it."

Perhaps to justify his defeat, Byers prophesied pessimistically of Longs Peak: "We are quite sure that no living creature, unless it had wings to fly, was ever upon its summit. We believe we run no risk in predicting that no man ever will be, though it is barely possible that the ascent can be made."

If Old Man Gun and his Arapahoes had bought the *Rocky Mountain News* that day, they would have smiled.

THE ROCKY MTN. SCIENTIFIC EXPLORING EXPEDITION.

Others tried to conquer the mountain. Some—including a Mr. Cromer of Gold Hill in 1860—claimed to succeed, but their confused geographical accounts did not lend much credence to their stories.

But the end of the Civil War released a major from the Union Army whose ambition and competence would steamroll the mountain's defenses. John Wesley Powell lost an arm in the Battle of Shiloh, but the Army had made a leader out of the naturalist. He spilled over with energy, with an unquenchable passion for exploring scientifically the half-civilized but still unstudied West.

Powell first came west in 1867. Professor at Illinois State Normal University, he brought his wife and a few students, climbed Pikes Peak, and looked around the Front Range. In 1868, he was back, with an expedition still mostly comprised of brothers and wives and volunteer college students, intent on collecting specimens for his Illinois museum—but also looking westward to an exploration of the Green and Colorado rivers.

In his definitive book on Powell and his era, *Beyond the Hundredth Meridian*, Wallace Stegner described their "Rocky Mountain Scientific Exploring Expedition": "Too late in time to be called explorers, too unskilled to deserve the name of frontiersmen, most of them strangers to the mountains, scientists only by an indulgent frontier standard. . ."

That summer Powell hired Jack Sumner, Middle Park mountain man and trader, as guide. Sumner happened to be William Byers's

brother-in-law, and Byers joined the group at Empire, with a mountain climber's gleam in his eye and a disappointment to avenge.

Stegner sums up Byers: ". . . a pioneer, an opener, a pass-crosser of a pure American breed, one for whom an untrodden peak was a rebuke and a shame to an energetic people." Powell—intent on the "unknown and untouched and undone"—made a perfect partner, bent on accomplishment and on harvesting knowledge of the new country.

They set up a base camp at Grand Lake, and a small climbing party began siege of the mountain August 20. It took two days of hard riding through tangled subalpine forest just to reach the western foot of McHenrys Peak, above today's Lake Powell. They climbed to the ridge leading from McHenrys over Chiefs Head Peak and Pagoda Mountain toward Longs, but soon decided this knife-edged arete was impassable. Retracing their steps, they moved over the Divide and into Wild Basin, south of the peak.

Here the group made camp between Sandbeach Lake and treeline about two in the afternoon, and examined the climbing route they hoped to follow the next morning. One line up the cliffs looked possible, and one of the young students, L.W. Keplinger, volunteered to go "in light marching order and reconnoiter" that afternoon.

Keplinger negotiated two tricky places, and found the summit temptingly close. When he wrote of that afternoon fifty years later, he remembered his thought: "Wouldn't it be a bully thing to go ahead and get a scoop on the other boys?" He went up and through the Notch, and onto the ridge above the East Face.

> All was well until I paused and looked down to my right on Estes Park. There, not to exceed ten feet below and away from me, was what seemed to be the eaves of the world's roof. I looked to my left toward camp, but the still unascended Peak was now between me and that. A lonesome feeling came over me. I started back.

Keplinger was shaken: ". . . never before and never since have I so completely lost all nerve. I was trembling from head to foot." He worked his way down toward camp in darkness, meeting the "halloing" Jack Sumner, sent up the mountain by Powell to light his way with signal fires. Keplinger not only found the way to the top, he came within 200 feet of the summit.

The next morning the group retraced Keplinger's route to below the Notch, where they cut left and ascended the same line followed by today's Homestretch. Byers's description of the Homestretch makes it sound more like the Diamond, but would match the reaction of many a nervous climber today: ". . . it required great caution, coolness, and infinite labor to make headway; life often depending upon a grasp of the fingers in a crevice that would hardly admit them."

By 10 A.M. on August 23, 1868, seven men stood on the summit

"... debris ... fell upon the ice with a crash. We did not linger ..."

Frederick Chapin, 1889.

of Longs: Major Powell and his brother Walter, William Byers, Jack Sumner, Keplinger, and two other students, Sam Garman and Ned Farrell. They built a monument, christened it with wine, drank the remainder (with two abstaining), and spent three hours on top, collecting plant and insect specimens and writing up their journals. Sam Garman almost tumbled off the edge trying to catch a butterfly. Keplinger produced a leaden biscuit baked by the Major at the last camp, intending to leave it in the summit monument "as an everlasting memento of Major Powell's skill in bread making." Powell insisted the occasion demanded more dignity.

As they were about to leave the summit, Major Powell "took off his hat and made a little talk." In Keplinger's words:

> He said, in substance, that we had now accomplished an undertaking in the material or physical field which had hitherto been deemed impossible, but that there were mountains more formidable in other fields of effort which were before us, and expressed the hope and predicted that what we had that day accomplished was but the augury of yet greater achievements. . .

Powell's prophesy came true for himself as for no other member of the little gathering. As Stegner puts it, from Longs Peak ". . . his vision of what might be accomplished must have expanded on that windy knob of rock as the view expanded below him. . ." He successfully completed his exploration of the Colorado River, broadened his survey to the whole of the Colorado Plateau, and invented stable, non-politicized government science in the form of the U.S. Geological Survey and Bureau of Ethnology. He came to understand the arid West better than anybody. Powell's climb of Longs Peak was both an end and a beginning.

TOURISTS, ROCKET SHIPS, *and* REV. LAMB'S SLIDE.

In the years surrounding Major Powell's climb, Colorado went through a whirl of civilizing. Longs Peak, in part because of its proximity to Denver, and in part by sheer force of personality, became a symbol of the newly pioneered territory. In 1866, when Jules Verne launched his fictional rocket ship from Florida in *From the Earth to the Moon*, he wrote of a 280-foot-high telescope built on the "summit of Long's Peak, in the territory of Missouri," where the director of the Cambridge Observatory tracked the missile's progress.

When travel journalist Bayard Taylor came through in 1867, he compared Longs Peak favorably with Mont Blanc. Taylor felt changes coming: ". . . I am doubly glad that I have come *now*, while there are

First to make Longs Peak his back yard, Elkanah Lamb homesteaded Tahosa Valley in 1876. In 1871 he made the first descent of the East Face—a wild ride down snowy "Lamb's Slide," today one of the primary climbing routes on the East Face.

Elephantella

still buffaloes and danger of Indians on the Plains, campfires to build in the mountains, rivers to swim and landscapes to enjoy which have never yet been described . . ."

Almost immediately after Powell's successful climb of the mountain, it became the favorite goal for adventurous Colorado tourists. In 1870, Donald Brown made the first climb via the Keyhole—the first solo ascent. Writer and scholar Henry Adams found Clarence King's U.S. Survey of the 40th Parallel working in Estes Park, and climbed Longs Peak with King in 1871.

The same year, the itinerant preacher Elkanah Lamb made his first Longs Peak climb. He had been proselytizing in the plains villages for the United Brethren, and for variety went on an excursion to Estes Park. His climbing vacation turned into the most spectacular mountaineering feat the mountain would see for thirty years.

Lamb's companions gave out before the Keyhole, and he went on alone, muttering something to them about having to "climb higher than this if we ever get to heaven." At the top, with his "mental and spiritual and somewhat poetical nature," he decided "to go down the eastern face of the mountain, where man had never gone before."

Reverend Lamb dropped to the Notch and began his descent, but after a thousand feet of downclimbing "began to realize the rashness of the undertaking." Retreat was impossible; he had already passed spots he could not climb up. He had no choice, so downward he went, negotiating Notch Couloir and then edging across Broadway to the long snowfield to the south.

> . . . I came to a place that seemed to say, "Thus far shalt thou go, but not farther." The mountain wall was not only perpendicular, but projected with a frowning incline some degrees over my icy pathway . . . With finger holds in meager niches of the wall and my feet pressing the edge of the ice, I started across this dangerous section. Quicker than I can tell it, my hands failed to hold, my feet slipped, and down I went with almost an arrow's rapidity. An eternity of thought, of life, death, wife, and home, concentrated in my mind in those two seconds . . .
>
> Fortunately for me, I threw my right arm around a projecting bowlder, which stood above the icy plain some two or three feet. This sudden stopping of my acrobatic performance brought my long walking appendages around with a musical swash, turning my overcoat skirts nearly over my head, and spilling all the specimens I had gathered on the summit . . . Getting my knife out of my pocket, I opened it with my teeth, then reached half-way to the rocks of safety and began digging a niche in the ice for a toe hold, when my knife broke in two . . . My nervous system was very much unstrung by this sliding, swinging experience, but I was compelled to decide— quickly, too. So putting the tip of my left foot in the shallow

In the early days, Longs Peak climbers rode horses to the Boulder Field before continuing on foot. One such adventurer said: "It makes little difference what route we choose across this field. One is as good—or as bad—as another."

niche I had cut, (knowing that if my foot slipped I was a lost Lamb,) then working my arm to the top of the rock, I gave a huge lunge, just managing to reach the foot of the mountain. . . I immediately fell upon my knees and thanked God for my deliverance . . .

No one would repeat "Lamb's Slide" until Enos Mills in 1903.

1873 : THE YEAR OF THE WOMEN.

Many climbers in the early 1870s wrote of their adventures on Longs Peak. But not until 1873 did a woman reach the top. Although Griff Evans and Enos Mills believed Anna Dickinson was first, Addie Alexander of St. Louis may have beaten her by a month.

Anna Dickinson was a strong personality: writer, lecturer, abolitionist, and actress. When she arrived in Estes Park, James Gardner of the Hayden Survey wasted no time in inviting her along on a Longs Peak climb. In these days before their consolidation as the U.S. Geological Survey in 1879, each of the four government surveys (led by Powell, King, Hayden, and George Wheeler) had to compete for limited Congressional funding. The more publicity they received, the better. Anna Dickinson may have been excellent company, but even if she had not, the Hayden men would have made sure the widely-known writer witnessed their glorious deeds.

Gardner and Ferdinand Hayden took along both Anna Dickinson and the indomitable William Byers on their September, 1873, climb. They had made a canny decision. In her account, *A Ragged Register*, Anna Dickinson wrote little of the climb and mostly of the geologists, "men who ought to be immortal if superhuman perseverance and courage are guarantees of immortality . . . braving rain, snow, sleet, hail, hunger, thirst, exposure, bitter nights, snowy climbs, dangers of death—sometimes a score on a single mountain"—all for "abstract science!"

Both Mount Meeker and Mount Lady Washington received their names on this trip. The former commemorates Nathan Meeker, founder of Greeley, whose son Ralph (a suitor of Miss Dickinson's) was along for the climb. Mount Lady Washington honors Anna Dickinson and her twenty-six climbs of New Hampshire's Mount Washington.

Two weeks later a small, courageous, cultured, and rather dumpy British woman rode steadfastly into Estes Park. Isabella Bird traveled "for recreation and interest solely," but her unflaggingly keen and objective eye on her solitary worldwide travels would lead to her 1892 induction as the first woman Fellow of the Royal Geographical Society.

69

Jims Grove—christened for Rocky Mountain Jim, who camped here with Isabella Bird in 1873. She said of this spot: ". . . when I call up memories of the glorious, the view from this camping ground will come . . ."

Anna Dickinson's wonderstruck hero-worship served well Hayden's political purpose. But Isabella Bird's clear-eyed description of her Longs Peak climb remains a classic—and still in print—more than a century later.

Isabella Bird stayed at Griff Evans's humble hostelry. But her heart was won not by the likable Evans but by Rocky Mountain Jim Nugent, trapper and desperado, half his face sheared away in a tangle with a grizzly, the other half a mirror of Shakespeare's aquiline profile. Griff Evans warned Isabella: "When he's sober Jim's a perfect gentleman; but when he's had liquor he's the most awful ruffian in Colorado."

Longs Peak entranced her:

> By sunlight or moonlight its splintered grey crest is the one object which, in spite of wapiti and bighorn, skunk and grizzly, unfailingly arrests the eyes. From it come all storms of snow and wind, and the forked lightnings play round its head like a glory. It is one of the noblest of mountains, but in one's imagination it grows to be much more than a mountain. It becomes invested with a personality.

Isabella Bird wished to climb Longs Peak, and she wanted Mountain Jim to guide her. Accompanying them were two young men with whom she had ridden up from Longmont. Isabella thought their manners abominable, much preferring Jim's incongruous courtliness. The two disinterested young climbers—law students out for a lark—"looked upon her somewhat in the light of an encumbrance." Later, when they read her book, they reckoned her differently.

Off they went one late September morning, riding to treeline the first day. In a last stand of spruce and fir forever after known as Jims Grove they camped, building a great bonfire. The men sang, Jim recited poetry "of his own composition, and told some fearful Indian stories." Then Isabella retired to a "bower of pines," with Jim's dog Ring at her back to keep her warm, to sleep "in the very heart of the Rocky Range, under twelve degrees of frost, hearing sounds of wolves, with shivering stars looking through the fragrant canopy, with arrowy pines for bed-posts, and for a night lamp the red flames of a camp-fire."

Jim said he had never seen a better sunrise than the dazzling beginning to their next morning. They left for the summit, with Isabella riding as far as the Boulder Field. She had borrowed a pair of Evan's boots, far too large, but on the way to the Keyhole she found a pair of small overshoes, presumably left by Anna Dickinson, which just lasted her the day. Isabella wrote that she felt "humiliated by my success, for Jim dragged me up, like a bale of goods, by sheer force of muscle." Jim decreed they would have to descend 2,000 feet below the normal route toward the Trough to avoid ice. "That part to me was two hours of painful and unwilling submission to the inevitable; of trembling, slipping, straining, of smooth ice appearing when it was least expected, and of weak entreaties to be left behind . . ."

70

Carlyle Lamb, Elkanah's son, led more than three thousand people to the summit, including New England mountaineer Frederick Chapin, who photographed him in Roaring Fork in 1887.

Jim succeeded in keeping her moving, past the "Dog's Lift" at the top of the Trough, where Ring refused to go on, along the Narrows, where "one slip, and a breathing, thinking, human being would lie 3,000 feet below, a shapeless, bloody heap!" Finally, the Homestretch, and then, the summit. All four were painfully thirsty, yet, "Uplifted above love and hate and storms of passion, calm amidst the eternal silences, fanned by zephyrs and bathed in living blue, peace rested for that one bright day on the Peak . . ."

"Gentle and considerate beyond anything," Jim hauled Isabella back to the Boulder Field, boosted her on her horse, lifted her off at camp, and laid her on the ground wrapped in blankets, "a humiliating termination of a great exploit." They spent a second night at Jims Grove, the law students asleep, Jim and Isabella sitting up by the fire. Jim told her of "a great sorrow which had led him to embark on a lawless and desperate life." As a proper Victorian she never reveals to us the depth of her feelings for him.

Isabella Bird took no false pride in her ascent: "Let no practical mountaineer be allured by my description into the ascent of Long's Peak. Truly terrible as it was to me, to a member of the Alpine Club it would not be a feat worth performing." Yet she spoke truly when she ended her account: "A more successful ascent of the Peak was never made . . ."

CLIMBING GUIDES *and* MOUNTAIN SPORTS.

The 1870s were eventful years for Estes Park. Windham Thomas Wyndham-Quin, the Irish Earl of Dunraven, hunted here in 1872, and returned in 1874 intent on appropriating the park as his private playground. In one dispute over Dunraven's tactics, Griff Evans, a Dunraven man, killed Rocky Mountain Jim, a member of the opposition, with a shotgun blast.

Dunraven commissioned the painter Albert Bierstadt to produce a huge $15,000 canvas of Longs Peak. Bierstadt's painting outlasted Dunraven's dreams of empire: the Earl built the first-class English Hotel in the late '70s, but left Estes Park for good in the 1880s. Today the painting hangs in the Denver Public Library.

Abner Sprague homesteaded Moraine Park in these years, making his first climb of Longs Peak in 1874. He found intact the baking powder can left by the first ascent party, complete with a photograph of Major Powell autographed by the seven climbers. When Sprague returned in 1878, vandals had riddled the historic photo with bullet holes. Sprague's brother Fred built the North Longs Peak Trail from Glacier Gorge up "their" side of the mountain.

*Longs Peak
by Thomas Moran.*

Elkanah Lamb returned to stay in 1876, having had enough of mission work. With his son Carlyle, he cut a wagon road through to Tahosa Valley and homesteaded the big meadow below Longs Peak. Parson Lamb had high hopes: "This location would seem to indicate more tangible and swifter strides to heaven than small salaries, partly paid in promises and hubbard squashes."

By 1878 the Lamb family lived in Tahosa Valley year-round, operating a dairy. They cut a steep pony trail to treeline on the mountain, setting themselves up for business as mountain guides at five dollars a head. "If they would not pay for spiritual guidance, I compelled them to divide for material elevation," declared Elkanah.

He had no lack of customers. The Reverend guided until about 1885. Carlyle guided from 1880 to 1902, making 146 trips to the summit and leading more than three thousand people. In 1880, he set out for the mountaintop with twelve members of the Longmont Cornet Band; six made it, including Al Cantonwine and his tuba. They played a brief program on top of Longs Peak, and Carlyle always claimed that folks at the ranch down in Tahosa Valley could hear the music.

When New Englander Frederick Chapin poked around Longs Peak during 1887 and 1888, Carlyle Lamb was his guide. Chapin's 1889 book *Mountaineering in Colorado* is a classic—he was the first to look at Longs Peak with knowledge of the beginning mountaineering tradition in Europe, with an eagerness to ascend new summits for the sheer sport of it.

Chapin eyed Longs Peak with a rock-climber's delight in routes:

> It has been rather fancifully named the "American Matterhorn;" but when we consider that one side is actually inaccessible, perhaps it is worthy the comparison,—for the Matterhorn has been ascended by *aretes* on all sides, though, of course, its easiest line of ascent is manifold harder to conquer than is the ordinary route of Long's Peak.

Chapin's favorite view of Longs was from Flattop Mountain, where "noble" Longs Peak looked "like a citadel perched upon enormous bastions and protected by ramparts made by intervening walls of rock." When he spent a night at the Lambs before his Longs Peak climb, Elkanah's stories around the blazing fireplace were so good that Chapin could scarcely sleep that night.

The next morning they reached treeline at "6.20 o'clock." Market hunters already had cleaned the lower slopes of game, forcing the herds deeper into remote country. Chapin remarked on the "splendid grass" of the tundra meadows that seemed to "go a-begging," for the cattle did not graze above the trees and "the deer, big-horn, and elk have forsaken this mountain for the northwestern peaks . . ."

Chapin judged the East Face "truly perpendicular," in the same class as those few "precipices" in Switzerland "which prove to be really worth the name." On their easy ascent of the Keyhole route, he decided that: "The difficulties of the ascent of Long's Peak are frequently exaggerated. There is hardly a place on the mountain where the climber need use more than one hand to help himself up." His detailed log of the climb was the first by an experienced mountaineer.

Yet Chapin showed great enthusiasm for the mountain, writing pages of praise for the summit views and the "grand outlooks" of the descent. Only oncoming darkness kept him from lingering longer in awe of the East Face, "as smooth as the side of Bunker Hill Monument . . . We should have to look to the walls about the Yosemite, to find anything superior . . ."

Carlyle Lamb also took Chapin to Chasm Lake, where the mountaineer/writer did his usual thorough job of speculating on glacial history and enthusing over the view. They skirted the lake "neither climbing nor walking; it was a continual jumping from slab to bowlder." The climbers traversed Mills Glacier. "While we were there, debris dislodged from a point half-way up fell upon the ice with a crash. We did not linger to investigate." However, they did place a line of cairns across the snow, returning two weeks later to see if there was "motion in that ice-stream." There was not.

Chapin combined a mountaineer's climbing passion with a naturalist's curiosity—and a bit of conservationist boosterism besides. He lingered long on the bouldery rim of Chasm Lake:

> . . . one sees the wide stretch of hazy plain, in appearance like the ocean in a calm, and can imagine himself back in the paleozoic age, when the great inland sea rolled to the westward before the mountains were uplifted and the waters retreated toward the gulf. . . . I would not fail to impress on the mind of the tourist that the scenes are too grand for words to convey a true idea of their magnificence. Let him, then, not fail to visit them.

Though Frederick Chapin made no mention of him, a teenager new to the mountains was helping Carlyle Lamb with trail work during the summer of 1886. This young man came to the area in 1884 and made his first Longs Peak climb in 1885. He must have relished every word of the fireside talks of Chapin and the Lambs, for he had the same endless fascination with mountains and their life—and Longs Peak in particular. His fascination would last for almost forty years.

His name was Enos Mills.

ENOS MILLS'S MOUNTAIN.

Enos Mills found his way to Longs Peak from his boyhood home in Kansas when he was fourteen. He had been sickly (evidently allergic to wheat), and his parents—gold rushers with fond

Enos Mills came to Longs Peak in 1884 and lived with the mountain for nearly forty years. From his little homestead cabin he determined to be "the best guide in the Rocky Mountains." Later he built rustic Longs Peak Inn and galvanized support for the creation of Rocky Mountain National Park.

memories of the mountains—encouraged him to seek health in the clear air of the Rockies.

Their plan worked. Enos spent the summer of 1884 in Estes Park, and returned the next year to work for Carlyle Lamb. He climbed Longs Peak for the first time, claimed his homestead, and began building a little cabin on it at the base of Twin Sisters. With the stubborn determination he showed throughout his life, and with the example of Carlyle Lamb to galvanize his dreams, Mills resolved to become the "best guide in the Rocky Mountains."

He built a life for himself from scratch. He climbed the mountain time after time, in all weather, seasons, and times of day. He began wintering in Butte, Montana, working as a miner to grubstake his summers on the mountain—steadily reading his way through the town's library. In 1889, with dozens of Longs Peak climbs under his belt, he began guiding on his own.

Another experience in 1889 gave new direction to his dreams; a fire closed the mine in Butte. With time on his hands, Mills traveled to California, where one day in San Francisco's Golden Gate Park he struck up a conversation with a fellow stroller who seemed to know much about the local vegetation. The man was John Muir.

Mills met Muir when he was nineteen, and the elder man passed on his conservation ethic to the awestruck young traveler. Mills adopted John Muir as his lifelong mentor. With Muir's encouragement he began to see himself as a man with a mission: to tell city people of the benefits of wilderness life—physical, mental, and moral—and convince them of the necessity to conserve wild country.

Longs Peak was his symbol, his classroom, and his home. Guiding in the summers, he worked winters in Butte for thirteen years until 1902, when he bought out the Lambs. He christened his new lodge Longs Peak Inn, and began transforming it into a center for what he called "nature study" as well as a business.

When the old lodge burned in 1906, Mills rebuilt it with fire-killed stumps harvested from Battle Mountain. The only finished wood was in the window casings and door. Tables sat on the roots of old trees. A latticework screen in front of the dining room turned out to be a cross section of an immense root system sixteen feet square. Paul Nesbit politely called the style "extreme rustic."

Enos Mills decided Longs Peak must be the focal point of a new national park. He made a powerful advocate: a zealous and eccentric idealist, implacable optimist, untiring storyteller, an expert mountaineer dedicated to propriety and self-improvement, yet bitterly adversarial with his enemies. Mills worked for two years as Theodore Roosevelt's Federal Lecturer on Forestry. He began touring the East each winter, telling his stories of beaver and grizzly, of riding out avalanches and

"Climbing the Peak before sunrise . . . The trail is a moon~toned etching."

Enos Mills, 1924.

At Enos Mills's Timberline Cabin, beds ran a dollar each, and the resident cook eased the challenge of summer climbers until the cabin closed in 1925.

coping with snow blindness.

Gradually, he added writing to his promotional skills. His books included tales garnered from 297 Longs Peak climbs. They told of guiding an eight-year old girl to the summit; of being blown up the Homestretch in gale-force "wind-rapids;" of butterflies "playing" in gentler winds in the Trough, floating up and then descending to do it again. He said of the mountain:

> . . . I think of it in a class by itself. . . . this towering and historic landmark of granite, old as the earth, will knit up the ravelled sleeve of care and enrich the imagination of multitudes.

Mills's years of wandering gave his stories the ring of truth. He was not the wise philosopher like Muir, but rather the popularizer of Muir's ideas. His books told a good yarn and included a wealth of detailed wildlife observations.

Enos Mills's intensity paid off. Year after year, he pushed for creation of a Rocky Mountain National Park. Though he first dreamed of a preserve stretching the length of the Front Range from Longs Peak to Pikes Peak, he gradually whittled at the ideal, making concessions to the possible. Over time, the battle became a conservation issue of national proportions. Finally, in 1915, after some six years of work aided by allies with crucial political savvy, Enos Mills served as master of ceremonies at the park dedication.

With his primary personal goal accomplished, he continued the outpouring of books from Longs Peak Inn—fifteen in all. Mills died in 1922, and his wife continued to run the Inn until 1945; the unique structure burned four years later.

Enos Mills treated Longs Peak as his private domain. Competing Tahosa Valley innkeepers at Hewes-Kirkwood and The Columbines were not pleased by his attitude. Charles Hewes, in fact, believed ravens did not live in the park until the first of the "ominous" black birds circled Tahosa Valley on the day Enos Mills died.

Nonetheless, until the park was created, Mills maintained the East Longs Peak Trail almost singlehandedly. Legendary guide Shep Husted, who climbed the mountain 350 times, surpassing even the lifetime total of Mills, said of his efforts:

> Mr. Mills did more to create an interest in mountain climbing than any one else in the Park. From 1888 to 1905, the years he was guiding, the trips increased from five or six parties a season to 75 or 80.

In 1908, Mills opened Timberline Cabin just below Jims Grove. Here ten climbers could spend the night in bunks (for one dollar each), buy meals prepared by a resident cook (at 75 cents per meal), and endure Enos Mills's commandment that men sleep in one bunkroom, women in the other. Longs Peak guide Harold Dunning described a night in the cabin:

> You were not expected to sleep for two reasons. First: Who in sam hill could sleep on a board, half froze, except a corpse. Second: There was always someone yelling, singing, fighting, complaining, cussing, preaching, pounding, or slamming the door. When morning came and you were supposed to be rested and fresh for a tough climb up Longs Peak, you were still weary and half dizzy from that night mare of a night you just went thru.

Enos Mills left his mark on the mountain. In his books, he ensured Longs Peak's reputation as a mecca for climbers and naturalists and documented its history and wildlife. He named Battle Mountain, Storm Peak, and Sandbeach Lake; others named for him Mills lake, glacier, and moraine. Above all, he led the fight to preserve this mountain in a national park, essential, he believed, for its ". . . room—glorious room—room in which to find ourselves, in which to think and hope, to dream and plan, to rest and resolve."

In 1921, Princeton mathematics professor James Alexander climbed the East Face solo and then climbed it again with crusty Rocky Mountain park ranger Jack Moomaw—the first publicized ascents of the East Face.

PROFESSOR ALEXANDER'S CHIMNEY.

When Roger Toll—shortly to become park superintendent—wrote *Mountaineering in the Rocky Mountain National Park* in 1921, he left the description of Longs Peak climbs other than the Keyhole route to Enos Mills, still the preeminent Longs Peak climber.

Mills described his 1903 retracing of Lamb's descent of the East Face. He told of winter ascents—his first, and the first for the mountain, also in 1903. Mills also seems to have been first up the North Face, first to climb Longs Peak from Mount Meeker, and first to describe climbs up the southwest and west ridges from the Keyhole trail (though he found evidence here of previous climbers).

The year 1921 also saw work begin on a new main trail up the east side of the mountain. The grade eased so much that the Chief Ranger could demonstrate its smoothness later that summer by riding a motorcycle to treeline. The next year, Ranger Mac Dings painted rocks along the Keyhole trail with the first "fried eggs." These yellow discs with red centers marked the route for people climbing without a guide (two-thirds of the total at that time). Not long before, a phone line had connected Timberline Cabin with Longs Peak Inn.

When ascent via the standard route became commonplace, the Colorado climbing elite began to eye the East Face. After two years of planning three members of the Colorado Mountain Club chose Labor Day, 1922, for their attempt at a first ascent. But two days before their climb, they awoke to read in the Denver morning paper that they had

Longs Peak climbers see the mountain's moods from the easy sunshine of the Boulder Field on a jaunty July morning to a white-out at the summit.

been scooped—on the very route they had planned.

Unknown to them, Professor James W. Alexander of Princeton University had spent several days with Park Ranger Jack Moomaw scanning the East Face for feasible routes. Nearly everyone rode to treeline or the Boulder Field in those days, so when Jack's horse was missing on the morning of September 7—the day of the planned Moomaw/Alexander summit attempt—the professor went on alone. He climbed the East Face solo, via Lamb's Slide, Broadway (which he named), and Notch Couloir.

Two days later, Alexander and Moomaw climbed the East Face together—again unroped. In his *Recollections of a Rocky Mountain Ranger*, Jack Moomaw, in his unique blend of understatement and braggadocio, said of the trip:

> In some ways I have regretted it, because for quite a time thereafter many climbers were killed attempting the feat. It also caused me a lot of hard work because afterward, every time there was an accident up there, they naturally assigned the job to me. . . . Many times I have been asked if I was not afraid on these climbs. Without boasting, I can honestly say that I was not, and that I never felt any particular thrills. This does not mean that I was not always very, very careful.

Their route followed "Alexander's Chimney" on the lower face and the Notch Chimney above Broadway. According to Moomaw: "Alexander later confessed to me that since early boyhood he had always had a terrible fear of high places; and that the first time he climbed Longs Peak, by the regular trail, he almost 'gave up' at the Key Hole. Here is something for the psychologists to mull over."

When the Colorado Mountain Club climbers Carl Blaurock, John L.J. Hart, and Dudley Smith arrived on September 10, they found a second group hoping to retrace Alexander's route. All joined forces, and Swiss-born Herman Buhl of this second group did most of the leading. His wife climbed, too—the first woman to climb the East Face. As they descended that evening, overdue, tired, stomping down in the dark, they met their determined rescuers—equipped with twenty-five-foot window sash cords.

Actually, even Alexander had been scooped. On August 23, 1919, the Longs Peak summit register showed this entry by Werner Zimmerman of Bern, Switzerland: "Alone. Traverse east west by abyss chimney 20 yards south." Zimmerman thus made the unpublicized first ascent of the East Face, perhaps by Alexander's Chimney, or further to the south, via the Longs-Meeker saddle.

The year 1922 marked a major transition for the mountain. Within the same month, Alexander conquered the East Face and Enos Mills died. Dominance of Longs Peak climbing passed from the pioneer resident guide to the visiting rock climber.

In the same year, another pioneer venture ended when the Eugenia Mine reverted to the park. Carl Norwall and Edward Cudahy discovered ore in 1905 on the lower flanks of Battle Mountain, and the Norwall family lived at the mine in a comfortable home complete with piano while they pursued their dream. By 1911 they had tunneled into a promising quartz vein over a thousand feet.

But like most hopeful prospectors in the West, the Eugenia miners did not find great riches here, and did not file on their claim after 1919. Today, a spur trail reaches the mine ruins (a boiler and several prospect holes) from the base of the East Longs Peak Trail.

Though thousands of people still climbed the mountain the "easy way"—and still do—Longs Peak *history* largely shifted to the East Face after 1922. Here happened many great deeds and great failures. The trail and Keyhole continued to see smaller successes—the personal milestones of newly minted mountaineers summiting their first great peak.

THE ICY DEATH OF AGNES VAILLE.

Many climbers have died on Longs Peak. But no death has been considered so tragic—nor had such lasting effects—as that of Agnes Vaille. An experienced climber and member of the tightly-knit Colorado Mountain Club, Agnes Vaille also was Superintendent Roger Toll's cousin. When she died after making the first winter ascent of the East Face with Walter Kiener in January, 1925, the city of Denver saw her loss as a civic tragedy.

Agnes made three attempts during the previous months, each time with Kiener, a Swiss-trained climber freshly immigrated to the United States, and once with the addition of East Face veteran Carl Blaurock. The three came within fifty feet of the summit ridge November 16, but a smooth slab of granite and oncoming darkness forced them back.

On January 11, Walter Kiener and Agnes Vaille tried again. They reached Timberline Cabin at 3:00 A.M.; at 9:00 the next morning they began the climb. Their companion Elinor Eppich headed down the mountain to await their return at Longs Peak Inn. The next morning, the two climbers had not appeared, and Elinor started a search. Four men from the Inn, Hugh and Oscar Brown, Jacob Christen, and Herbert Sortland, headed up to Timberline Cabin.

Soon after their arrival, Walter Kiener staggered in from the gale, with a desperate story to tell.

Kiener and Vaille climbed all day on the eleventh and then kept on through the night. A storm blew in and dropped the temperature far below zero, blasting the mountain with one hundred mile an hour

Agnes Vaille and Walter Kiener reached the summit via the East Face for the first time in winter. Kiener photographed their stormy ascent on January 12, 1925. But the climb ended in tragedy: the memorial hut at the Keyhole pays respect to Agnes Vaille, who perished on the descent, and to Herbert Sortland, who died attempting to rescue her.

winds. When they reached the summit at 4 A.M. on the twelfth, their hands were too frozen to sign the register. They continued directly down the North Face, the shortest escape route. Agnes, after 25 hours of steady climbing, slipped. She slid 150 feet, unhurt, but she was completely exhausted. Kiener, though a powerful man, had no strength left to carry her. He got her down to the base of the North Face, left her in as protected a spot as possible, and raced for help—on frozen feet.

And now he was returning as promised. Agnes was alive when he left her at the head of the Boulder Field, but they must get to her as fast as they could. Oscar Brown stayed behind at the cabin to keep the fire blazing. The other four set off into the blizzard.

Fierce winds turned back Hugh Brown quickly; at the cabin Brown sent his son down the mountain for more help. Herbert Sortland nearly made it to Granite Pass, but also had to turn back. Kiener and Christen struggled on to where Agnes Vaille's body lay. She had moved about a hundred feet, but lay face down, her arms outstretched, killed by cold and exhaustion: hypothermia. In leading the snowblind and frostbitten Kiener back to Timberline Cabin, Christen saved his life.

After dark, three rangers reached the cabin. One was Jack Moomaw, who described the scene:

> On entering the cabin we found three men, Kiener, Hugh Brown, and Christen, huddled around the stove with the lids off to keep the fire from all going up the stove-pipe. The cabin was almost half full of snow and a lot of the wind was passing right through the cracks in the log walls. A loose piece of roofing tin was flapping with an awful din at one corner of the roof. Of course we inquired for Miss Vaille, and one of the men told us that she was dead up on the Peak. They then wanted to know if we had met Sortland and Oscar Brown on our way up. When we told them that we had seen nothing of the two boys, they looked mystified.

The men spent a miserable night in the cabin. Brown and Christen went down during a lull; Superintendent Toll and Edmund Rogers (Toll's hand-picked heir as superintendent) arrived at 4 A.M., icicles hanging from their chins and noses. Moomaw slit the blisters of Kiener's painfully frozen hands. Finally they all returned to the Inn, where Kiener was taken to a hospital and the rest waited for days until the storm cleared enough to retrieve Agnes Vaille's body.

Oscar Brown had made it down safely. But Sortland became lost in the blizzard, and his body was not found for weeks, melting out of a snowbank just three hundred yards from the Inn. He had broken a hip and must have crawled down the mountain, crossing—and missing—the road in the storm.

Walter Kiener lost parts of every finger but one, all his toes, and part of one foot. Later, he returned to the mountain to study tundra

The Boulder Field Shelter Cabin and horse barn operated from 1927 to 1935—at 12,700 feet, the "highest hotel in the world."

vegetation and serve as the Twin Sisters fire lookout. He made his first climb after the tragedy mostly on elbows and knees. Carl Blaurock summed up the tragic events: "What a price to pay for a stubborn and, I think, foolish venture! Two lives lost and a crippled survivor."

Roger Toll had a similar reaction. But as the man charged with the safety of climbers on the mountain, he set about doing something about his sorrow.

HIGHEST HOTEL IN THE WORLD.

Toll declared an "urgent need" for shelter cabins on Longs Peak to help prevent disasters like the Agnes Vaille winter ascent. In the summer of 1925 he set to work.

When Esther Mills, Enos's widow, announced her plans to shut down Timberline Cabin that summer, Roger Toll proposed building a new cabin and stable in the Boulder Field itself. Jack Moomaw was his field lieutenant. Moomaw supervised the extension of the phone line up to the Boulder Field (coating the wire in creosote to prevent marmots from eating the insulation), rebuilt the trail from Timberline Cabin to the Boulder Field, and placed the famous iron cables on the North Face.

Jack Moomaw and his trail crew did such a good job of making the Boulder Field trail look "as though it has always been there," that it was hard to believe they packed up over two tons of dynamite—and used it. The cable installation, actually easier work, received most of the attention.

When Walter Kiener proposed the cables after his climb with Agnes Vaille, Roger Toll agreed that such a permanent "handrail" might help climbers. Moomaw again went to work, later suspecting: "I sometimes think they had it in for me." The first day he stationed his two crew members below to keep hikers away, and went up the North Face with a crowbar to clean the route. "This was a safety measure for ourselves and for the people who would later use the cable. Such a rock-rolling opportunity comes but once in a lifetime, and it was something to watch."

They drilled holes, cemented eyebolts, and then they were ready. Moomaw and his crew:

> . . . uncoiled the cable, placed the men a few feet apart with the cable over their shoulders, and lugged it up like a long snake to the cliff face, where we fed the front end through the eye-bolts. After this, it took only a little time to screw on the clamps. And there it was.

Kiener complained to Toll that the two hundred feet of cables should have been closer to the East Face, "so the climbers could get

more of a thrill." Moomaw disagreed. He "went up and had a look." "I was not thrilled; I was just plumb scared."

Work on the shelters took more time. Agnes Vaille's father donated money to build a small hut at the Keyhole. It stands there today, a memorial to the deaths of Vaille and Sortland, but too tiny and cold to offer protection from storms. The main shelter cabin became Toll's pet project; both the Vaille hut and the shelter cabin were begun in 1926 and completed in 1927.

Fourteen by eighteen feet inside, with two-storied double walls of masonry filled with rubble, the labor required to build the cabin impressed guide Harold Dunning:

> . . . after two years of hard work a roof was finally built that would stand the wind. Three times it blew off and was scattered over that thousand acres of rock. Wind up in that amphitheatre is as good as dynamite for it can blow things all to smithereens and then stop and be as quiet as if nothing had ever happened. Great timbers were imbedded in rock and cement across the top of the building and then the roof nailed and wired on to the timbers. Then tons of rock were piled on top of the roof afterward and finally it stayed.

Joe and Paul Stettner headed west from Chicago on a climbing vacation in 1927. They first spotted the Rockies from far out on the plains and went on to climb Longs Peak by the most difficult route yet, Stettners Ledges.

Still, each winter the shelter filled with ice. Every spring, a crew had to clear it for the two and one-half month summer season. The horse barn fared better: its detachable roof was removed off-season.

On completion, guide Robert Collier leased the shelter, opening for business what Ripley's "Believe It or Not!" christened "the highest hotel in the world," at 12,700 feet. Collier officially could sleep 12 on his straw ticks, but could scarcely turn people away in bad weather. At least once, fifty climbers spent the night in the shelter and barn.

Lodging ran two dollars per person each night. Meals ranged from $1.25 for breakfast to $1.75 for dinner. Guide service up Longs Peak (ascending the cables, descending by the Keyhole) cost $2.50 per person, in parties of four or more.

THE REMARKABLE STETTNER BROTHERS.

In September of 1927—the autumn after completion of the Boulder Field shelter— Joe and Paul Stettner loaded their gear on vintage Indian motorcycles and headed west in search of mountains. The two (26 and 21 years old respectively) had climbed in their native Bavarian Alps before immigrating to Chicago, but the Midwest only offered a few rocks to play on. Five bouncing, dusty days later they sighted mountains—real mountains. They had one in particular in mind.

The Stettners knew of Alexander's Chimney and Kiener's "mountaineer's" route via Lamb's Slide and Notch Couloir. But they hoped to pioneer a new East Face route. They brought with them pitons and carabiners from Europe—state-of-the-art equipment as far as Colorado was concerned. For a rope they had to settle for the Estes Park General Store's finest hemp.

Their vacation was limited and they wasted little time. On September 14 they left Timberline Cabin, climbed to Mills Glacier, and, as Joe wrote years later, began looking for a new route:

> About 200 feet to the right of Alexander's Chimney we noticed some plates, cracks, and ledges leading to Broadway, and that looked challenging enough for us. We had some reservations regarding some spots that looked icy, but Paul said, "We can worry about that when we get there."

Paul was unstoppable. Once changed from hob-nailed boots to felt-soled climbing shoes, he immediately started the climb unroped, leaving Joe with the heavy knapsack. "I had to ask him how he went so I could catch up with him. Once I was close to him, I said, 'All right, you lead, but take the rope and put it on, and keep it on. . .'"

And so the two moved up through what came to be called Stettners

Ledges. Paul led, catching Joe in a fall at one particularly nasty place, negotiating the places that first looked impossible with pitons for protection. "In good time and in good shape" they reached Broadway. Then they climbed quickly on to the summit. The whole climb took just six and one-half hours.

Satisfied for the time being, the Stettners cycled back to Chicago. Paul's motorcycle broke down in Sterling, Colorado, and Joe towed him all the way to Omaha with their climbing rope.

Their lightning-fast visit to the mountain remained unknown to most people. Only a few Longs Peak devotees knew of it. The climb sounded innocuous enough in their straightforward description, but it marked a great leap forward. In the next twenty years, Stettners Ledges saw only two successful climbs, one of them led by Joe Stettner.

Bob Godfrey and Dudley Chelton rate Stettners Ledges in *Climb!*, their history of rock climbing in Colorado:

> In 1927 it was the most difficult Colorado high mountain rock climb and probably the most difficult in the United States. [Only Albert Ellingwood's 1920 ascent of Lizard Head, in the San Juan Mountains, came close.] No other climbs were to occur in Colorado until the mid-1940s surpassing them in daring and technical difficulty.

THE GLEEFUL THIRTIES. The 1930s

may have brought a great Depression to the United States, but they brought carefree times to Longs Peak. While Robert and Dorothy Collier operated the Boulder Field Shelter Cabin from 1927 through 1935, guides working for Collier scampered up and down the mountain on easy routes with paying customers, and on harder and harder routes to entertain themselves (though none as difficult as Stettners Ledges). Judged safer than ever, the mountain saw 2,132 signatures in the summit register in 1931, the largest number until 1954.

Each year the *Estes Park Trail* enthusiastically announced the opening of the hostel and "the long, long Longs Peak trail." Throughout each summer the paper chronicled many of the climbs. One 1931 issue celebrated the Timberline Telephone Service, which kept this ". . . desolate, almost inaccessible spot—only a half-mile from Europe via phone." *The Trail* proclaimed: "While Longs Peak is said to be the seventh hardest climbable peak in the world, it is said to be the fifth most interesting from a scenic standpoint."

From the top of the peak, the guides set off Fourth of July fireworks visible from as far as Fort Collins. They rounded out the 1931 season by climbing the East Face for the first time at night, accompanied by Mrs. Collier (completely recovered from a lightning strike at the cabin in

"*The last two miles ... too rough to be ridden ... 'is above burro line.*'"

Enos Mills, 1924.

1929). The same year, Ev Long dashed from the Boulder Field to the top in 34 minutes; his record return was seventeen minutes. Clerin Zumwalt made 53 summit climbs in 1932. In 1927 the first marriage took place on the summit—in a June snowstorm.

At the end of each season, Bob Collier would tally up the summit register, close the shelter about Labor Day, and depart for his winter teaching job in Denver.

Paul Stettner returned in 1930 with his new wife Anne, who had never climbed a mountain. He hauled her up Alexander's Chimney according to *The Trail*, and branched out onto the face.

> Several times Mrs. Stettner slipped and swung at the end of the rope, but her cool companion always drew her up to safety on a higher ledge. Those at Boulder Field who knew of the intended climb sat on the rim of the chasm all day, thrilling to the spectacle.

Joe Stettner paid a solo visit in 1936. He claimed a route to the left of Notch Couloir so difficult that modern climbers believe he must have been on easier ground farther left. Joe, alone and unroped, found it "very hard and felt that I took chances on it." If a Stettner said that, it was hard indeed, and may well have been the route Joe marked on photos.

The guides showed almost as much enthusiasm for the mountain in winter. In February, 1934, Clerin Zumwalt, with Charles Hardin, made the first winter ascent of the East Face since Vaille and Kiener. A series of News Years Day climbs begun by Jack Moomaw in 1928 climaxed when Edwin Watson made the first solo East Face winter ascent in 1939.

Rescues made for adventures, too. Jack Moomaw tells of several close calls on Mills Glacier, retrieving crumpled bodies fallen from the East Face while rocks came zinging down around them. As he put it laconically, "It was easy to understand what had killed the man we were carrying."

Mac Dings remembered an earlier retrieval of a man killed by lightning on the summit. Below the Homestretch and headed for Moomaw's pack horse in Wild Basin, they were caught by a lightning storm while lowering the body, wrapped up "like a mummy." Dings called it one of the eeriest experiences of his life.

Longs Peak winters got the better of the Shelter Cabin by 1935, its last year of operation. Riven by frost, its roof blown off one last time, the Park Service demolished the building in 1937. The barn was removed in 1959.

Walter Kiener lamented the loss of the cabin in a 1936 edition of *The Trail*. He guessed that no more than one-fifth of the 1936 climbers hiked with paid guides, and remained earnestly concerned about the lack of "necessary shelter against the rigors of the climate and unexpected fatigue of hikers." But he also noted the omens of a new era:

> . . . a most remarkable change had taken place with the closing of the shelter house. Gone from the Boulder Field was the atmosphere of commercial exploitation, gone the profanity, gone the grazing donkeys and the vicious dogs. More wildlife was reported by the visitors than ever before. For the first time the Park Service detailed a summer ranger for the exclusive patrol on Longs Peak. . . . It is probable that the absence of shelter made people conscious of the need for better co-operation and more friendliness.

The quiet mountaineer's mountain described by Kiener in 1936 has changed little—except for the numbers of those mountaineers. But the *climber's* version of Longs Peak has been overthrown and re-invented a dozen times. Technical climbers considered Stettners Ledges the ultimate challenge before World War Two: Climbing the Diamond was unthinkable, impossible.

But techniques and hardware—and climbers themselves—keep getting better and better, ensuring, in Bob Godfrey's and Dudley Chelton's words, "the continual redefinition of that most ubiquitous of rock climbing assertions . . . 'Impossible!' " After the 1940s, the story of Longs Peak becomes the story of rock climbers. They made climbs of the "impossible" Diamond first possible, then "casual."

Sunrise from the top of Longs Peak, when earth and sky meet— and connect.

The rhythm of climbing: clanking hardware, the echo of signals shouted between partners, and the tedious hauling of bags of gear. An overhang slows the leader, and the second climber gets a chance to photograph. Night brings bivuoacs, welcome relaxation of adrenaline and rest.

This great mural of subtle hues turns into a background—though an overwhelming one—with the addition of even a single climber.

The next morning:

> . . . we had to make a crucial decision, as our fixed line ran diagonally upward and outward to the left. We could leave a fixed rope from the upper bolt to the bivouac ledge. Otherwise, when we stepped into our prusik loops and swung into space, retreat would be impossible. Should we cut off our retreat and find that the water-flowing upper chimney was impassable, it would be up to our support party to help us.

Choosing to cut off retreat, they moved on. They negotiated the icy chimney and reached the top of the Diamond at 1:15 P.M.

The sheer competence of Kamps and Rearick, and the other climbers who would follow them up the Diamond, disguises the incredible adventure of what they do. When they write about the climb, bold and exhausting moves over hair-raising exposure come across as laconic, technical summary.

We can feel with Elkanah Lamb the whoosh of cold air and the biting crystals of the snow as he slides down the mountain. We can struggle on through the cold blast of a blizzard with Agnes Vaille. But the Diamond remains the accomplishment of its climbers in a uniquely personal way.

They come down from the mountain with grins, but with few words. Rearick and Kamps describe a possible bivouac ledge above the "ramp . . . 18 to 24 inches wide, quite level, and about 15 feet long." They advise the next party to "have a generous supply of angle pitons of the inch and larger variety." They state that they placed four bolts for belay and rappel anchors, not for direct aid. But they waste no words on whys and wonderings. Royal Robbins has said: ". . . we climbers are endlessly asked by nonclimbers, 'Why do you climb?' The proper answer is, 'If you have to ask, you'll never understand.' "

The world below the cliffs, however, remains determined to partake vicariously in the adventure of the Diamond. Though reporters dashing up and down the mountain during the Kamps-Rearick climb wrote most vividly about their own hardships, the two climbers were feted everywhere from the Estes Park Rooftop Rodeo Parade to TIME Magazine.

The Diamond was an ultimate—the biggest, highest, steepest, most tantalizing wall in the Southern Rockies. To the non-participating watchers below, its first ascent was a magnificent conquest—a word climbers themselves hesitate to use.

Another word that climbers avoid is "impossible." They hungered after the impossible Diamond, climbed it, then repeated the climb time after time. Non-climbers size up such an undertaking and say, "out of the question."

Layton Kor spoke for all climbers each time he discovered a difficult and unlikely new route and said flatly, "It's *got* to be climbed."

LIVING TO CLIMB.

Layton Kor dominated Longs Peak climbing in the 1960s, as he dominated climbing throughout Colorado. At 6'5", radiating nervous energy like sparks, and with inner drive unmatched by any other climber, he made first ascent after ascent, and negotiated rock more rotten than anyone else would dare.

Newspaper articles about his exploits always identified him as "a Boulder bricklayer." That was his trade, but he lived to climb, and the 1960s introduced to Colorado a new breed who made climbing a way of life. Kor's immense talent and legendary eccentricities made him a leader of this group. Refined techniques made impossible climbs possible.

Unclimbed walls lay waiting throughout the state, and the climbers who went after these firsts had personalities that bred stories. The decade was Colorado's Golden Age of climbing.

Kor climbed with Ray Northcutt on the Diagonal. In 1962 he made the second ascent of the Diamond, on a route he named the Yellow Wall, roping in Charlie Roskosz, a member of his support team, when the two registered climbers became ill. Charlie's wife did not know he was climbing until she read it in the newspaper on the second day of the climb.

Paul Nesbit dramatized this climb, and his scene of Roskosz seconding a lead by Kor gives a good feel for the sounds of the climber's ritual. Sit at Chasm View on a summer's day and listen to the echoes across the great space nudging the rock wall:

> "On belay," shouted Kor, now anchored to the rock beside him and giving the signal that he was braced against any possible fall and ready to take up the rope as Roskosz climbed. "Climb," he shouted after a tug on the rope allowed him to feel the security of his position.
>
> "Climbing," replied Roskosz as he started upward, avoiding the use of the rope as a climbing aid. There were scraping noises from movements against the rock, grunting, puffing, knocking of pitons back and forth as he worked to get them out; metallic releasing noises as they came, and tinkling, jangling noises as he snapped them and carabiners to the piton belt about his waist.
>
> Up to Kor and a careful, cautious changing of positions. The jangling hardware is handed over to Kor who is now eager for exercise to get his blood to circulating more actively again. The signals continue: "On belay." "Off belay." "Climb." "Climbing." "Slack" (more rope needed). "Up rope" (pull up slack). "Tension" (keep rope tight). Throughout could be heard the rising pitch of the "pings" of the pitons as they were driven in, or the "bongs" of the larger, lower-pitched bong bongs for wider cracks.

The next summer Kor spent a couple of remarkable climbing days

Layton Kor, "excited and unrestrained, usually moving, usually climbing on rock or in life."

on the Diamond with Royal Robbins, one of the elite of Yosemite climbers. The two pushed each other hard, climbing the Kamps-Rearick route (called D-1) in one long sixteen-hour day. Robbins wrote later:

> I knew there was no one in the country, perhaps in the world, at that moment, with whom I stood a better chance of climbing the Diamond in one day than with Layton Kor. . . . Climbing with Kor, one could not remain unaffected by his tumultuous energy. It was stressful, because to climb with him as an equal required that one function at the limit of one's abilities.

Two days later, they climbed in similar record time a new route which they named Jack of Diamonds.

That fall Layton Kor was back on the mountain, climbing a number of new routes on the lower East Face with Tex Bossier. They did the Diagonal Direct, without the traverse used up to that time—in a straight line up the angled crack from Mills Glacier to Broadway. Where the traverse struck right, a storm caught them, and their climb became a deadly race against the wrathful weather of Longs Peak. Rain funneled water down the crack system they were pioneering. It began to turn to snow, fog rolled in, and the wall started to ice up. Both Kor and Bossier knew they had to get off the mountain that day.

They sprinted for Broadway. An avalanche swept Kor out of his stirrups, backwards. They started leaving pitons in place, and then, after reaching Broadway, even abandoned a rope that got stuck—anything to make time. When Bossier fell while traversing Broadway, Kor's emergency belay could never have held him, but one leg stayed on the ledge. Climbing on what Bossier called a "constant pumping of adrenaline the whole time," they made it to Chasm Lake Shelter:

> Next day we looked up and could see the wall. It was encased in ice. It was completely frozen over. If we'd been up there, we'd just have been a goddamned icicle along with everything else. I said to Kor afterwards, "I don't think I would have made it if we'd had to stay the night up there." Kor replied, "Yes you would. You'd have made it if I had to stay up all night and beat on you with my hammer." But the way he said that, I also had the feeling that he didn't know for sure whether he would have made it or not.

Pat Ament climbed the Overhang Dihedral below Broadway with Kor in 1964:

> . . . the harsh stone was not the life. Rather it was Kor, molding a personal and living experience from solitary places . . . eluding the probable and defying the fragile. . . . Kor had his madness in the Sixties, but also serenity . . . a bright and searching spirit, a sort of wild form, excited and unrestrained, usually moving, usually climbing, on rock or in life.

END OF THE GOLDEN AGE.

What do you do when the Diamond has been climbed, not once but by several routes? You climb it in winter, risking some of the worst weather in the mountains. And then? Climb it alone.

Wayne Goss and Bob Culp had trouble talking Layton Kor into attempting the Diamond in winter. But Culp and Goss were persuasive, and Kor joined them for their second winter attempt on the Diamond in March, 1967.

Bob Culp turned back at Broadway with a sore throat. Kor and Goss continued in six inches of fresh snow, spending a miserable night on Broadway. After two pitches, they left fixed ropes and retreated to Chasm lake Shelter Cabin to wait for the storm to clear.

The weather relented, and Goss and Kor returned to the mountain a few days later. In two days of climbing they forced their way to the top via a new route, the Enos Mills Wall. Both nights caught them climbing by headlamp. But down sleeping bags and clothing kept them "reasonably comfortable" where forty years earlier and a few yards to the south, on a similar night Agnes Vaille and Walter Kiener has been powerless to prevent their hands and feet from freezing.

Kor wrote of their second night on the climb:

> Once again darkness set in and as our headlamps were giving us trouble, we almost expected a night in slings on the blank wall . . . Fifty feet above, another large roof provided a strenuous ten minutes and a spectacular view into the depths. Above the overhang the crack widened . . . After many minutes of struggling with rope slings and my headlamp cord I somehow managed to force several pitons deep into the icy crack, setting up the last belay of the climb. Wayne soon shared my position at the hanging "spaghetti gardens."
> . . . I led into the night with a blinking headlamp until the wild blast of the wind told me it was all over. We arrived at the top of the wall at about 10 P.M. and bivouacked on the spot.

This was one of Layton Kor's last major climbs. In his foreword to Kor's autobiography, *Beyond the Vertical*, Royal Robbins envisions Layton looking ". . . out and off into the distance, and as far as he could see stretched an endless range of mountains. I can imagine Layton eyeing those peaks receding into infinity and seeing in them insufficient food to satisfy deeper hungers." In 1968, Kor gave up climbing and turned to religion to satisfy his remarkable inner drive.

Still, the Diamond beckoned to those climbers who sought adventure in high places. Gradually the National Park Service eased restrictions as Diamond climbs became more commonplace. They dropped the requirement for a backup team and in 1970 legalized solo climbing. A new race was on for the next "first."

Big mountains are made of ice as well as rock, and Longs Peak's frozen waterfalls train climbers for ventures in still higher places—Alaska and the Himalayas.

Classic Diamond Climbs:

1) Broadway
2) Kieners
3) Diagonal Direct
4) The Window
5) Window Direct
6) Diagonal

7) Table Ledge
8) D-7
9) Yellow Wall
10) Forrest Finish
11) Overhang Dihedral
12) Casual Route

13) D-1 (Kamps-Rearick)
14) North Chimney
15) Jack of Diamonds
16) Enos Mills Wall
17) Hornbein Crack
18) Old Cable Route

Several climbers failed in their solo attempts as Denver climber Bill Forrest quietly went about training to reach his personal peak.

"When soloing," Forrest reflected, "the keen sensations experienced while climbing with a partner are intensified. Using a hold, testing a piton, choosing the route—critical moves and decisions—become super-exciting and meaningful. There is an absolute premium on successful execution. And successful execution is largely a matter of preparation."

Forrest carried all his own gear—eighty pounds worth—up to the climb, rappeling from Chasm View to Broadway on July 23. On the Diamond he belayed himself by tying into his rope with a friction knot (a Heddon knot) that would hold tight under the pressure of a fall. At the top of each pitch, he put in a belay anchor, descended, and climbed back up, cleaning his route of pitons. In the Sixties, mechanical ascenders called jumars replaced prusik knots; while climbing, Forrest also clipped one of these onto his rope as double-insurance in tight places.

On the first day he climbed four pitches of Kor and Roskosz's Yellow Wall and set up a hammock bivouac, swaying in the breeze 1,500 feet above Chasm Lake.

> Long before dawn, I was awakened by a terrible roar as an avalanche of rock cascaded down the north chimney. Sparks shot through the darkness and the mountain seemed to groan and lurch, but my anchors held and the bottom didn't rip out of my hammock. I couldn't get back to sleep, and I hung in the chilly breeze waiting for the beautiful sunrise.

The next day he began forging a new route. Not far up he came to "an evil crack—too wide to jam, too narrow to chimney. I cursed, prayed, chickened out, and finally got with it and struggled . . . That crack took my best, but once up it, I was glad I was there . . ."

Easier climbing led to his bivouac on Table Ledge. Eight feet wide, it granted an easy night. Forrest left a few peanuts out to munch on, and awoke in the dark eye-to-eye with a pika feasting on his snack. On other Diamond routes, Forrest could slip into womblike chimneys and escape for a few moments from the exposure of the face. But this route offered no such respite. The next day he continued the delicate task, balancing caution, concentration, and confidence. He completed "Forrest's Finish to the Yellow Wall" by noon.

The Stettners culminated the Twenties with the boldest climb in the era of primitive equipment. Forrest's climb brought to a finish the era that began after World War Two, with the invention of direct aid and the refinement of sophisticated ropework and pitoncraft.

But master climbers never seem to stay on any plateau of accomplishment for long. Dangling in stirrups from the heights, comfortable with the big walls, they proceed to reinvent their rules once again.

Approaching the mountain in winter.

The mountain does not always forgive poor judgment. Surprise storms create havoc with even the most careful climbers. Whether saving lives or participating in tragedy, Longs Peak rescuers face difficult work.

THE FREE CLIMBERS.

As the Sixties faded into the Seventies, climbers returned to basics, refining free climbing—feet and hands always on the rock, with never a reassuring lunge for metal. Hard steel pitons banged in and out of popular routes caused new concerns, for they left the walls looking like roughed out sculpture. Hexagonal nuts began to replace pitons. Easily jammed into cracks without need for a hammer, they left the rock unscarred and provided adequate protection along with permanently fixed pitons.

Climbing historians speak of the eras of conquest, of difficulty, and of style. For Longs Peak, the era of conquest may have encompassed only the first ascent of the mountain by Powell and his group; perhaps Alexander's solo of the East Face qualifies. Next came the long era of "climbs of difficulty," with climbers choosing tougher and tougher routes, but willing to use any technology necessary to ascend them.

Finally, the carefree use of direct aid to "get to the top" gave way to an all-encompassing sense of style. Climbers strove to repeat aid climbs, but without relying on pitons or nuts as holds. New footgear with flexible smooth rubber soles replaced stiff-soled mountain boots. They hurt like hell, but they made a connection from foot to rock that felt close enough to pass as spiritual. Free climbers dusted their holds with chalk to maximize their grip—though purists dismissed this as "direct aid." Gymnast/mountaineers, they got better and better on the short, difficult pitches around Boulder. The Diamond, of course, was next.

Starting in 1972, the young "hot shots" began to make free attempts on D-7, the easiest and shortest route on the Diamond, first climbed in 1966 with direct aid. For three years they failed to free climb the whole route, repulsed on each effort by a system of wet cracks about midway. But in July, 1975, Wayne Goss and Jim Logan, two "old-timers" active mostly in the Sixties, trained to a high standard of free climbing and headed for the Diamond.

They traveled light, taking no hammers, pitons, or jumars. They carried minimal bivouac gear and food. Luck was with them as far as Broadway: they found Molly Higgins, Stephanie Atwood, and Laurie Manson camped there, intent on making the first all-female ascent, with direct aid. The women had the full complement of gear and at dinner shared their hamburger feast. The next day the slower aid climbers acceded first rights to the fast-moving pair of free climbers.

The two men bypassed the wet cracks by moving off D-7 to the Forrest Finish and a difficult, but dry, pitch. Rain caught them about the time they began to feel less than fresh. Goss led the crucial pitch below Table Ledge, moving onto the face around a dirt-filled crack:

> The climbing is no worse than before, but I am . . . Some hero, squinting because it's too wet to wear glasses, reaching across a gulf of fear to deliberately finger an eighth-inch indentation just two fingers wide. Which ones to put there? Decisions, decisions. Left foot lifts off the pucky in the crack, and with pluck defying better judgment, belaying a mind of its own, replaces the right. Right is relegated to a newer, but not better, bump. This is art? . . . Switch fingers one at a time. Contrapuntal elegance. Left foot slides—up, now or never, and place it under the same side's fingers . . . in slow motion cartwheel upwards thinly . . . a vertical hold slips by . . . "Got it!"

Both Logan and Goss climbed every pitch. The Diamond had been climbed free. And on that same day, the three women made the first all-female Diamond ascent. A year later, Roger Briggs and Bob Candelaria extended the Logan and Goss route from Table Ledge directly to the summit—claiming a free ascent of the *entire* Diamond."

Free climbers also began pushing at another frontier, solo climbs. Some of the hardest of the low-cliff Boulder routes yielded free solos—not solos with complicated self-belay systems, but solos done without ropes. When Charlie Fowler heard about a new route on the Diamond so easy it was called the Casual Route, he knew he could solo it. In July, 1978, he did just that, climbing the Diamond for the first time alone, without a rope—in an hour and a half.

Since then several climbers have made successful solo winter ascents (using direct aid). Mark Wilford did a "total" winter ascent, climbing both the lower wall and the Diamond; the Czech Thomas Gross spent 17 days on the Diamond during his winter climb. John Harlin III skied from the summit down the North Face in May, 1983. And most of the major Diamond routes have been climbed free, including D-1.

Whatever you can do, or dream you can, begin it. Boldness has genius, power, and magic in it.

Goethe.

*   *   *

Longs Peak is two mountains—one of rock and tundra, home to plants and creatures, balanced in the fragile and dynamic moment of the present. A second mountain exists, within human experience, a great rock wall where each climber unites with the implacable bulk of the peak in graceful movements over granite, transcending the mere physical for that same fleeting moment.

Beyond each of these moments, the mountain prevails, without regard for climbers, glaciers, or time itself.

Given the history of impossibilities made possible, we would be foolish to think that nothing new remains to be done on Longs Peak. Think of a new way to climb the mountain. Call it impossible. And dare climbers to prove you wrong.

Wait a while. Someone will.

MOUNTAIN WITHOUT BOUNDS

WHAT distinguishes Longs Peak from every other mountain?

Not just its size or height or verticality. Nor simply the drama of its location, commanding a hundred miles of plains.

All of these in combination influence the mountain's stories. They make Longs Peak remarkably distinct. Colorado mountaineering historian William Bueler says: ". . . no other mountain in the West—not even Mt. Rainier or the Grand Teton—has a more interesting history."

For rock climbers, the Diamond is unique, demanding their best—at 14,000 feet. They mumble about the "long" approach hike; other 1,000-foot rock climbs begin a few yards from roads. Still, they revel in the mountain as well as its rock. To Bill Forrest, the most memorable images from the Diamond have been the sunrises—never such sunrises.

Finally, Rocky Mountain National Park protects Longs Peak. This fact makes a huge difference for the mountain. Park designation also draws attention—and enormous crowds. Some 10,000 people a year try for the peak. The summit register filled up so fast that the park finally removed it after 1976.

We have the same need to understand the role of national parks in our country as we do the place of the mountain in our lives. Both are important, but full of paradox and conflict. How do we manage a safe climb of Longs Peak, but maintain enough of its adventure to keep it meaningful? How much can we develop a national park and still leave its wilderness qualities intact?

In some ways, we have chosen to make Longs Peak literally a "mountain without handrails," to borrow the title from Joseph Sax's fine book on national park ethics. Our philosophy has changed since the days of Roger Toll. In 1969, the Boulder Field phone line was dismantled. The missing wooden door on the Agnes Vaille hut has not been replaced, clarifying its function as a memorial, not a shelter. In 1973, the National Park Service removed the cables from the North Face.

The cables created a bottleneck; with vast increases in numbers of climbers came hour-long waits above 13,000 feet. More and more Longs

Peak hikers lacked experience, and the cable route posed a danger by misleading with its supposed ease. The steel cables marred the mountain with permanent "artificial aids." This last reason for their removal mirrored the transition from climbing with slings and bolts to free-climbing protected by nuts.

People are the mountain's main problem. The parking area at the base of the trail fills up soon after dawn on busy summer weekends. Thousands of hikers and climbers leave behind contaminated water and tons of raw sewage. Trampling has so damaged sensitive, slow-growing alpine meadows that Jims Grove was closed to camping in 1984.

Beginning in 1983, only overnight Diamond climbs required registration with park authorities—and then only for a backcountry camping permit issued alike to hikers luxuriating in tents and climbers spending the night dangling in bivouac hammocks.

Edward Abbey protested in *Desert Solitaire* against overprotective rules in national parks:

> A venturesome minority will always be eager to set off on their own, and no obstacles should be placed in their path; let them take risks, for Godsake, let them get lost, sunburnt, stranded, drowned, eaten by bears, buried alive under avalanches—that is the right and privilege of any free American.

Why are we eager to take such risks? Why do we climb mountains? Why do some of us push to our absolute limit, put our lives on the line in some "impossible" way that no one has ever done?

Climbing Longs Peak, climbing any mountain, edges us closer to the answers, but they hover in tantalizing ways around the experience. The answers lie sleeping in a subalpine meadow, and glittering in the tremble of aspen leaves. They are not tied in a neat bundle and waiting in the summit cairn.

Being with a mountain is simple. But understanding its simplicity is difficult. We do not conquer the mountain; it does not submit. Rather, we conquer and reveal something within ourselves. We prove that our limits still lie out there somewhere, beyond where we have gone.

And so we keep trying to learn something about the mystery of being alive by venturing to the edge of that mystery. But each time, the rock still feels sharp and hard and warmed by the morning sun. It feels understandable.

The mystery lies beyond where we can go.

In our wanderings over the mountain we can reclaim our intimacy with other creatures and feel a rare communion with the land. Perhaps this is mystery enough.

In *Everest: The West Ridge*, Tom Hornbein wrote of setting out for the summit of Mount Everest with Willi Unsoeld on the last day of their climb. He stood above 27,000 feet and tried to connect what he felt with the rest of his life:

> I snugged a bowline about my waist, feeling satisfaction at the ease with which the knot fell together beneath heavily mittened hands. This was part of the ritual, experienced innumerable times before. With it came a feeling of security, not from the protection provided by the rope joining Willi and me, but from my being able to relegate these cold gray brooding forbidding walls, so high in such an unknown world, to common reality—to all those times I had ever tied into a rope before: with warm hands while I stood at the base of sun-baked granite walls in the Tetons, with cold hands on a winter night while I prepared to tackle my first steep ice on Longs Peak. This knot tied me to the past, to experiences known, to difficulties faced and overcome. To tie it here in this lonely morning on Everest brought my venture into context with the known, with that which man might do. To weave the knot so smoothly with clumsily mittened hands was to assert my confidence, to assert some competence in the face of the waiting rock, to accept the challenge.

We accept the same challenge whether we stroll in Longs Peak forests, make our first trip through the Keyhole, or free climb a new Diamond route. We choose to be with the mountain and to live with the consequences of our choice.

Longs Peak knows no bounds. It balances infinite possibility with perceived impossibility. We walk the invisible boundary between the two when we climb the peak—or dream of climbing the peak.

Over a century ago, Isabella Bird saw Longs Peak as "much more than a mountain." She was right.

Longs Peak rises above Denver's skyline as a refuge and a beacon. It grants a crucial balance to the city and its people; freeing our spirits each time we look up to it.

APPENDIX I: *CLIMBING RATINGS*

In his *Climbers Guide To Rocky Mountain National Park*, Walt Fricke sums up the Kamps-Rearick route up the Diamond (D-1): V, 5.7, A4. He gives the following route description for the third lead of the Diagonal:

> Diagonal up and right 20 feet (fifth class) back into the crack system, and go up it some 70 feet (A1 and A3), then do a layback (variously rated as 5.6, 5.8, or aid) up to a grassy platform some ten feet below an overhang. 130-140 feet in all.

These ratings obviously are written in a foreign language. Here is a brief translation.

The Roman Numeral refers to the overall size of a climb, the magnitude of the commitment. It measures the amount of time the imaginary "average" climber should plan for a climb. Thus:

I: Two hours or less; about two leads, or less than 300 feet of climbing.

II: Two to four hours; up to five leads, or 500 feet of climbing.

III: Most of a day; several hundred feet of climbing.

IV: All day or a little more than a day. Be prepared to bivouac.

V: Definitely more than a day.

VI: More than two days on a big wall (two or more bivouacs).

The Keyhole ranks as Grade I. Stettners Ledges and The Window are Grade II climbs. Old-fashioned Diamond climbs with a mixture of free climbing and aid are Grade V.

The second parts of climbing ratings are the confusing numbers spawned by the Yosemite Decimal Rating system. This system defines six classes of climbing:

1:    Hiking on a trail.

2:    Off-trail scrambling.

3:    Extremely easy climbing. Inexperienced climbers need a rope for protection but experienced climbers do not.

4:    Most people climb belayed.

5:    Technical climbing; leader places anchors for protection.

6:    Direct aid.

With all hard free climbing lumped in fifth class, subdivisions soon arose, from easiest 5.0 to difficult 5.9. As climbers got better, they began doing moves harder than 5.9. Since the next official decimal, 6.0, was preempted by aid climbing, the harder moves became 5.10, and then 5.11, 5.12, and incredibly, 5.13.

The classic encyclopedia of climbing *Mountaineering: The Freedom of the Hills* describes these categories in understandable terms:

5.0 to 5.4:   There are two hand- and two footholds for every move; the holds become progressively smaller as the number increases.

5.5 to 5.6:   The two hand- and two footholds are there, obvious to the experienced, but not necessarily so to the beginner.

5.7:   The move is missing one hand- or foothold.

5.8:   The move is missing two holds of the four, or missing only one but is very strenuous.

5.9:   This move has only one reasonable hold which may be for either a foot or a hand.

5.10: No hand- or footholds. The choices are to pretend a hold is there, pray a lot, or go home.

5.11: After thorough inspection you conclude this move is obviously impossible; however, occasionally someone actually accomplishes it. Since there is nothing for a handhold, grab it with both hands.

5.12: The surface is as smooth as glass and vertical. No one has really ever made this move, although a very few claim they have.

5.13: This is identical to 5.12 except it is located under overhanging rock.

Finally, there is a classification for the security of direct aid placements on the route, which breaks down sixth class climbing into five categories:

A1:   Good protection.

A2:   Could hold a short fall, if necessary.

A3:   Holds the weight of the climber in stirrups, but would not hold a fall. Piton or nut difficult to place.

A4:   Will hold body weight if the climber stands very gingerly.

A5:   Four or more A5 anchors.

Try reading Fricke's ratings and route description again. They should make sense now.

One last note: the official rating ranks the hardest move and the most insecure protection. A climb ranked "5.9, A4" may have only one move and pin placement this extreme. Complete route descriptions clarify the overall difficulty of the climb.

APPENDIX II: *NOTABLE LONGS PEAK FIRSTS*

1868 John Wesley Powell led the first documented climb to the summit on 23 August, via the South Face from Wild Basin. His party included L.W. Keplinger (who scouted the route), William N. Byers, Walter Powell, Jack Sumner, Ned Farrell, and Sam Garman.

1870 Donald Brown made the first solo climb, via the Keyhole.

1871 Elkanah Lamb made the first descent of the East Face.

1873 The honor of being first woman to climb Longs Peak seems to go to Addie Alexander of St. Louis, but Anna Dickinson's climb in September received more publicity.

1885 Enos Mills made his first Longs Peak climb.

1896 First moonlight climb, by H.C. Rogers in August.

1903 First winter ascent, by Enos Mills in February. Mills also made the first ascent of the North Face near this time.

1919 Werner Zimmerman's first ascent of the East Face on 23 August, probably via Alexander's Chimney, the Eighth Route, and Gorrell's Traverse.

1922 Professor James Alexander of Princeton made the first publicized ascent of the East Face on 7 September. On 10 September, Mrs. Herman Buhl became the first woman to climb the East Face. Mac Dings marked the Keyhole Trail with "fried eggs."

1925 First winter ascent of the East Face, by Walter Kiener and Agnes Vaille on 12 January. Agnes Vaille died on the descent. That summer, Jack Moomaw directed the completion of the Longs Peak Trail and phone line to the center of the Boulder Field and the placement of cables on the North Face.

1927 First marriage on top of Longs Peak: Lucille Goodman and Burl Stevens, 14 June. Joe and Paul Stettner climb Stettners Ledges, 14 September.

1931 First one-legged climber, Francis W. Chamberlin, climbs to the summit with crutches. First night ascent of East Face by Ev Long, Carleton Long, Melvin Wickens, and Dorothy Collier.

1939 First solo climb of East Face in winter, by Edwin Watson.

1950 Bill Eubanks and Brad Van Diver made the first ascent of the Window.

1959 Ray Northcutt and Layton Kor climbed the Diagonal.

1960 First ascent of the Diamond on 3 August, by Bob Kamps and David Rearick.

1963 First one-day Diamond ascent, Layton Kor and Royal Robbins.

1967 Wayne Goss and Layton Kor made the first winter ascent of the Diamond in March.

1970 First solo Diamond ascent, by Bill Forrest.

1975 Jim Logan and Wayne Goss free-climb the Diamond to Table Ledge.

1976 Roger Briggs and Bob Candelaria free-climbed the entire Diamond.

1978 First solo Diamond free ascent (unroped) by Charlie Fowler.

1983 John Harlin III skied the North Face.

APPENDIX III: *DEATHS ON LONGS PEAK*

1. Carrie J. Welton; Waterbury, Connecticut; 23 September, 1884

According to Enos Mills, Carrie Welton was "an eccentric, cultured, and wealthy young lady, who had given enormous sums of money to the Society for the Prevention of Cruelty to Animals." Carlyle Lamb, her guide, suggested turning back at the Keyhole, but she insisted on continuing. By the time they returned to the Keyhole from the summit, she collapsed from exhaustion. "At her urgent request," Lamb left her at about 9:00 P.M. and went for help. When he returned near dawn, she had died from exhaustion and overexposure.

2. Stryker boy, 24 years old; Tipton, Iowa; 28 August, 1889

Carlyle Lamb guided the Stryker family (father, son, and two uncles) to the summit, where two of the men practiced target shooting with their pistols. Descending between the Homestretch and Keyhole, the son's pistol—loaded and in his pocket—went off when he bumped a rock and mortally wounded him in the neck.

3. Gregory Aubuchon, 18 years old; Michigantown, Indiana; 20 July, 1921

The Aubuchon family was preparing to leave the park when Gregory asked to climb Longs Peak. They said no, but he snuck away on their last night in Glacier Basin Campground and was not seen again until September, when rangers found his body on Mills Glacier. He evidently fell from the North Face or the summit.

4. H.F. Targett, 55 years old; Los Angeles, California; 26 September, 1921

Targett told the Longs Peak Inn manager that he was planning a hike to Chasm Lake. No trace of him was found until a skull believed to be his only remains turned up near Peacock Pool nineteen years later.

5. J.E. Kitts; Greeley, Colorado; 21 August, 1922

Kitts was standing on the summit about 12:30 P.M., when a sudden storm swept through and a bolt of lightning struck and killed him. A man standing next to him had his head seared and his shoes burned off.

6. Agnes Vaille, 31 years old; Denver, Colorado; 12 January, 1925

After successfully climbing the East Face with Walter Kiener for the first time in winter, Agnes Vaille collapsed at the foot of the North Face and died of hypothermia before Kiener could return with help.

7. Herbert Sortland, 22 years old; Litchfield, North Dakota; 12 January, 1925

Caretaker of Longs Peak Inn, Sortland died during the attempted rescue of Agnes Vaille. Last seen when he turned back at Granite Pass, Sortland became lost in the blizzard, broke his hip in a fall, and froze to death within 300 yards of the Inn. His body was not found until late February.

8. Forrest Keatring, 19 years old; Denver, Colorado; 23 July, 1926

In the Notch Chimneys, Keatring lost his footing and fell a thousand feet to his death. He was climbing with others—all unroped.

9. Charles Thiemeyer; Denver, Colorado; 18 August, 1929

Thiemeyer was climbing with two other Swiss-born climbers above Broadway on the East Face. He was leading, tied to a 30-yard rope held by his partner below. He fell, the rope slipped through the fingers of his friend, and Thiemeyer did not live to regret his earlier comment that there were "no mountains in Colorado worth climbing."

10. R.B. Key; Lake, Mississippi; 18 September, 1931

Key's body was found at the base of the East Face, evidently killed in a fall. Rangers identified him by a time slip in his pocket.

11. Robert F. Smith; Michigan City, Indiana; 18 July, 1932

Pausing on the Cables to enjoy the view, a rock fell from above and struck Smith in the head. He was killed instantly.

12. Gary Secor, Jr., 16 years old; Longmont, Colorado; 29 August, 1932

Son of a prominent Longmont lawyer, Secor left his partners on the descent and attempted a shortcut through the False Keyhole. He took a 150-foot fall and died before help could be brought up the mountain.

13. John Fuller; Ames, Iowa; 8 August, 1938

Fuller told friends he was going up the North Face to try out his new boots. Another party saw him next, hurtling end over end with a small avalanche following him. He landed at the base of the North Face on the snowfield called "The Dove."

14. Gerald Clark, 37 years old; Denver, Colorado; 7 August, 1939

Clark first climbed the peak against family orders in 1920 and climbed many dangerous routes over the succeeding years. On his last climb he became stranded in Field's Chimney on the East Face after climbing an overhang against advice, using up his rope, and losing the head of his piton hammer. His friends went for help, and Clark spent the night on the ledge in 26-degree weather and in a spray of water from above. A small rock hit him during the rescue. Dazed by the rock and weakened by exposure, he died as rangers lowered him down the East Face.

15. Charles Grant, 19 years old; Chicago, Illinois; 1 September, 1946

On Stettners Ledges, Grant reached out to grab a rope and save his falling partner. He missed the rope and fell to his death. His partner was saved by the rope after a 60-foot fall.

16. Earl F. Harvey, 19 years old; Gretna, Virginia; 5 June, 1954

After ascending the cables in considerable snow, Harvey's party tried to descend along the ridge above the Keyhole. He plunged 500 feet to the snowfield below the North Face, and skidded to the Boulder Field, dying of his injuries.

17. Rena Hoffman, 33 years old; Chicago, Illinois; 15 August, 1956

A bolt of lightning struck Rena Hoffman while she walked along Mills Moraine, killing her instantly.

18. David L. Jones, 18 years old; Webster Groves, Missouri; 20 April, 1960

Four University of Colorado students tried an off-season climb. One turned back early, but the other three made the summit where a storm forced them to bivouac. One eventually made it out, after being helped down the South Face by Jones. Jones fell trying to rope down later, his hands too frostbitten to handle the ropes.

19. Prince D. Willmon, 23 years old; Fort Smith, Arkansas; 20 April, 1960

Willmon led the climb mentioned above. He fell about 400 feet, Jones 1,000 feet, both over precipices below the Homestretch on the South Face.

20. Ken Murphy; Kingfisher, Oklahoma; 27 August, 1962

Ahead of his party at the summit, Murphy apparently missed the main trail on his descent, and fell about 100 feet onto ledges above the Keyhole route. He died of head and neck injuries.

21. James Scott O'Toole, 20 years old; Pasadena, California; 30 September, 1962

Climbing alone, O'Toole attempted a shortcut from the Keyhole to Chasm View. He fell over the cliffs and onto the snow of The Dove.

22. Blake Heister, Jr., 48 years old; Denver, Colorado; 27 August, 1966

Leading a four-man party up Kieners Route on the East Face, Heister started unroped up the Notch Chimney to find the route when he slipped and fell 1,200 feet. His body was retrieved from 250 feet down the bergschrund at the head of Mills Glacier.

23. Rudolf Postweiler, 48 years old; Boulder, Colorado; 11 September, 1971

Postweiler sat down on a rock about three miles up the Longs Peak Trail, complaining to his friends of breathing problems. He had a heart attack, lost consciousness, and died on the spot.

24. Fred Stone, 20 years old; Minneapolis, Minnesota; 23 January, 1972

Fred Stone and Joan Jardine tried to ski to Chasm Lake, but were caught in a blizzard. They left their skis near Jims Grove, and evidently walked from there. Stone may have fallen near the lake and sent Jardine for help. His pack and sleeping bag were found near Peacock Pool. His body was not located until the following August, in lower Roaring Fork.

25. Joan Jardine, 21 years old; Fort Collins, Colorado; 23 January, 1972

Stone's companion walked down Roaring Fork valley to within a half-mile of Highway 7. On the fifth day of the search her body was found next to a large boulder, where she had attempted to bivouac or rest.

26. Paul Russell, 24 years old; Lincoln Park, Michigan; 12 June, 1972

Leaving his companion at the Keyhole, Russell pushed on through ice and snow without technical equipment. He fell to his death at the east end of the Narrows.

27. Jay Van Stavern, 19 years old; Boulder, Colorado; 1 April, 1973

After climbing the East Face, Van Stavern and his partner were working down from the summit toward the cables when Van Stavern slipped and fell all the way to Mills Glacier.

28. Michael G. Neri, 21 years old; Estes Park, Colorado; 1 June, 1977

Traversing Broadway unroped and with a 70-90 pound pack, Neri slipped on wet tundra and fell to Mills Glacier.

29. Harvey Schneider, 22 years old; Boulder, Colorado; 16 September, 1978

Schneider, with ice axe and crampons but no hard hat, fell on Lambs Slide, sliding to the bottom and dying of massive head injuries. His group had not roped up because they were not experienced and were afraid that if one slipped they would all go.

30. Dr. Edward Sujansky, 43 years old; Denver, Colorado; 1 September, 1979

After a successful climb, Sujansky died of a heart attack at the Keyhole.

31. Charles Nesbit, 36 years old; Golden, Colorado; 6 October, 1979

Cramponing unroped up Lambs Slide, Nesbit slipped and fell to his death.

32. Kris Gedney, 22 years old; Boulder, Colorado; 14 November, 1979

Gedney, depressed about his performance on his medical school entrance exam, among other things, drank six times the fatal dose of antifreeze, and jumped off the Narrows, falling 200 feet. His suicide note consisted of two handwritten Psalms left in his pack.

33. Robert Siver, 16 years old; Cedar Rapids, Iowa; 26 June, 1980

Climbing with his boy scout troop and a local guide, Siver panicked on the Homestretch. He got into trouble, hanging only by his hands, slipped, and began to run downhill in an effort to regain his balance. He fell and hit his head, dying of his injuries.

34. Robert Elliott, 27 years old; Eldorado Springs, Colorado; 10 January, 1981

A "Friend"—a mechanical cam anchor—placed by his climbing partner, came loose and Elliot fell 90 feet down North Chimney until caught by his rope. He died of spinal injuries.

35. James Duffey III, 24 years old; Marshall, Colorado; 16 December, 1981

After an East Face climb, Duffey and his partner (the same climber that survived the Elliott tragedy) were forced to bivouac on the summit. The next day, suffering from hypothermia, they headed down the Keyhole route, which neither had climbed. Duffey refused to go on at the top of The Trough, and his partner felt he had to keep moving to survive. He left him, made it down, and sought help, but a storm kept rescuers off the route for two days. They found Duffey's body 200 yards from the Keyhole.

SUGGESTED READINGS

MOUNTAIN GEOLOGY

Chronic, Halka, 1980. *Roadside Geology of Colorado*. Mountain Press Publishing, Missoula, Montana.
Cole, James C. 1969. "Geology of East-Central Rocky Mountain National Park and Vicinity, With Emphasis on the Emplacement of the Precambrian Silver Plume Granite in the Longs Peak-St. Vrain Batholith." University of Colorado Ph.D. dissertation.
Curtis, Bruce F., ed. *Cenozoic History of the Southern Rocky Mountains*. Geological Society of America Memoir 144.
Flint, Richard F. 1971. *Glacial and Quaternary Geology*. John Wiley & Sons, New York.
Harris, David V. 1980. *The Geologic Story of the National Parks and Monuments*. John Wiley & Sons, New York.
Ives, Jack D., ed. 1980. *Geoecology of the Colorado Front Range: A Study of Alpine and Subalpine Environments*. Westview Press, Boulder.
Richmond, Gerald M. *Raising the Roof of the Rockies*. 1974. Rocky Mountain Nature Association, Estes Park, Colorado.

Richmond's book still provides the best introduction to park geology, though the dates of his glacial chronology no longer are accurate. Chronic places the park in perspective within the state. For more technical papers, see Ives and Curtis. McPhee offers a fascinating and entertaining piece on how geologists think, and on the revolution in the science brought about by the concept of continental drift.

MOUNTAIN ECOLOGY

Armstrong, David M. 1975. *Rocky Mountain Mammals*. Rocky Mountain Nature Association, Estes Park, Colorado.
Benedict, Audrey D. 1985. *A Sierra Club Naturalist's Guide—The Southern Rocky Mountains*. Sierra Club Books, San Francisco.
Kiener, Walter, 1967. *Sociological Studies of the Alpine Vegetation on Longs Peak*. University of Nebraska Studies: New Series 34, Lincoln.
Marinos, Nic and Helen. 1981. *Plants of the Alpine Tundra*. Rocky Mountain Nature Association. Estes Park, Colorado.
Mills, Enos. 1923. *The Adventures of a Nature Guide*. Doubleday and Company, New York.
Mutel, Cornelia F. and John C. Emrick. 1984. *From Grassland to Glacier: An Ecology of Boulder County, Colorado*. (Second Edition). Johnson Publishing Company, Boulder.
Nelson, Ruth Ashton, 1982. *Plants of Rocky Mountain National Park*. Rocky Mountain Nature Association. Estes Park, Colorado.
Peet, Robert K. 1981. "Forest Vegetation of the Colorado Front Range: Composition and Dynamics." *VEGETATIO* 45: 3-75.
Weber, William A. 1976. *Rocky Mountain Flora*. Colorado Associated University Press, Boulder.
Willard, Beatrice E. 1979. "Plant Sociology of Alpine Tundra, Trail Ridge, Rocky Mountain National Park, Colorado." *Colorado School of Mines Quarterly* Volume 74, Number 4, Golden.
Zwinger, Ann. 1970. *Beyond the Aspen Grove*. Random House, New York.
Zwinger, Ann H. and Beatrice E. Willard. 1972. *Land Above the Trees: A Guide to American Alpine Tundra*. Harper and Row, New York.

Benedict provides a comprehensive regional introduction (and also covers geology and climate). Zwinger and Willard tell the story of the tundra. For more technical information, see Peet, Willard, and Kiener. Ives, cited in *Mountain Geology*, also includes ecological papers. To identify Longs Peak plants, use Nelson and Weber.

HISTORY

Arps, Louisa Ward and Elinor Eppich Kingery. 1977. *High Country Names: Rocky Mountain National Park*. Rocky Mountain Nature Association, Estes Park, Colorado.
Bartlett, Richard A. and William H. Goetzmann. 1982. *Exploring the American West, 1803-1879*. National Park Service Handbook 116, Washington, D.C.
Bird, Isabella L. 1879. A Lady's Life in the Rocky Mountains. Reprinted 1977 by Comstock Editions, Sausalito, California.
Buchholtz, C.W. 1983. *Rocky Mountain National Park: A History*. Colorado Associated University Press, Boulder.
Cassells, E. Steve. 1983. *The Archaeology of Colorado*. Johnson Books, Boulder.
Dunning, Harold. 1956. *Over Hill and Vale*. Privately published, Boulder.
Marsh, Charles Seabrooke, 1982. *People of the Shining Mountains: The Utes of Colorado*. Pruett Publishing Company, Boulder.
Moomaw, Jack C. 1963. *Recollections of a Rocky Mountain Ranger*. Times-Call Publishing Company, Longmont, Colorado.
Randall, Glenn. 1981. *Longs Peak Tales*. Stonehenge Books, Denver.
Rippeteau, Bruce Estes. 1979. *A Colorado Book of the Dead: The Prehistoric Era*. Colorado Historical Society, Denver.
Sage, Rufus B. 1846. *Rocky Mountain Life*. Reprinted 1982 by University of Nebraska Press, Lincoln.
Stegner, Wallace. 1953. *Beyond the Hundredth Meridian: John Wesley Powell and the Second Opening of the West*. Houghton Mifflin, Boston.
Wild, Peter. 1979. *Enos Mills*. Boise State College Western Writers Series, Boise, Idaho.

Curt Buchholtz introduces every aspect of park history in his comprehensive book. For regional perspectives, start with Bartlett and Goetzmann. Many of the quotes in my text from early sources—or citations of those sources—can be found in Buchholtz, Mills, or Arps & Kingery. Glenn Randall's book takes several crucial events in Longs Peak history (including climbing tales) and retells them as historically accurate short stories.

CLIMBING

Bueler, William M. 1974. *Roof of the Rockies: A History of Mountaineering in Colorado.* Pruett Publishing Company, Boulder.

Chapin, Frederick A. 1890. *Mountaineering in Colorado.* W.B. Clarke and Company, Boston.

Dannen, Kent and Donna. 1982. *Rocky Mountain National Park Hiking Trails—including Indian Peaks.* The East Woods Press, Charlotte, North Carolina.

DuMais, Richard. 1981. *The High Peaks.* Ridgeways, Boulder.

Fricke, Walter W., Jr. 1971. *A Climber's Guide to the Rocky Mountain National Park Area.* Privately published, Boulder.

Godfrey, Bob and Dudley Chelton. 1977. *Climb!: Rock Climbing in Colorado.* Alpine House, Boulder.

Hornbein, Thomas F. 1965. *Everest: The West Ridge.* Sierra Club Books, San Francisco. Reprinted 1980 by The Mountaineers, Seattle.

Kor, Layton (Bob Godfrey, ed.). 1983. *Beyond the Vertical.* Alpine House, Boulder.

Nesbit, Paul W. 1946 (and subsequent editions). *Longs Peak: Its Story and a Climbing Guide.* Privately published, Colorado Springs.

Peters, Ed, editor. 1982 (Fourth Edition). *Mountaineering: The Freedom of the Hills.* The Mountaineers, Seattle.

Tobias, Michael Charles and Harold Drasdo, eds. 1979. *The Mountain Spirit.* The Overlook Press, Woodstock, New York.

Wilson, Ken. 1978. *The Games Climbers Play: A Collection of Mountaineering Writing.* Sierra Club Books, San Francisco.

Godfrey and Chelton's book tells the history of Longs Peak climbing in broad perspective; the book's wealth of detail is incredible and the black-and-white photographs superb. Nearly all the climbers's quotes in my text appear in their book or Bueler's. Kor's book has finely-printed color photos of his Longs Peak climbs. Tobias and Drasdo look at mountains from a spiritual and philosophical stance. Hornbein's book is a classic of mountaineering literature written by an important Longs Peak climber.

CONSERVATION

Abbey, Edward. 1970. *Desert Solitaire: A Season in the Wilderness.* Simon and Schuster, New York.

Sax, Joseph L. 1980. *Mountains Without Handrails: Reflections on the National Parks.* University of Michigan Press, Ann Arbor.

CREDITS

PHOTOGRAPHS

Carl Blaurock collection: page 80
Lou Daken: page 98
Kent and Donna Dannon: pages 7, 8, 26, 52 (dryas) & 87
The Denver Public Library, Western History Department: pages 1, 22, 51, 58, 60, 65, 72 & 92
Peter Dunmire: pages 15 & 52 (clover)
James Frank: pages 28, 31 & 61 (bottom)
Bob Godfrey & Dudley Chelton (from CLIMB: ROCK CLIMBING IN COLORADO): pages 77, 84
     & 96
Bob Jamieson: pages 13, 67, 91, 93 (lower right) & 95
Lee Jamieson: page 94
Tim Lucas: page 30 (ponderosa trunk)
National Park Service: pages 11, 40, 42, 43, 44, 49, 52 (rose crown), 54, 66, 67, 69, 71, 74, 76, 78,
     81 (b/w), 82 (both), 85 & 86
    Joe Arnold, Jr.: pages 14, 52 (columbine), 100 & 102
    Ferrel Atkins: page 17 (top)
    Chase: page 46 (top)
    George Cowles: pages 43 & 74 (Longs Peak Inn)
    Mike Donahue: pages 34, 47, 52 (top), 79, 90, 93 (left) & 97
    Glenn Dunmire: page 100
    Bob Haines: pages 12, 17 (bottom), 20 & 74 (cabin)
    George Hockman: pages 18 & 48 (left)
    Glen Kaye: pages 14 & 48 (center)
    Charlie Logan: pages 89, 93 (top & upper right) & 101
    Stewart Schneider: page 48 (right)
    Frank Smith: page 16
    Kenneth Smith: page 88
Cherry Payne: page 99
Stephen Trimble: cover, title spread, pages 21, 25 (both), 27 (both), 30 (cones), 32, 35, 36, 38 (both),
     39, 52 (meadow & pika), 53, 61 (top), 70, 81 (both), 104, 105
United States Geological Survey: page 64

ILLUSTRATION CREDITS

Dean Babcock (from SONGS OF THE ROCKIES): pages 13, 29, 55, 89, & 103
Marj Dunmire: pages 24, 57, & 68
Merrill J. Mattes collection: page 83
Samuel Seymour: cover inset & page 56